# The Long Walk Home

### How I Lost My Job as a Corporate Remora Fish and Rediscovered My Life's Purpose

## James Brian Kerr

**Blydyn Square Books**
Kenilworth, New Jersey

*For my parents*

© 2022 by James Brian Kerr

ISBN 978-1-7322567-3-6 (paperback)

ISBN 978-1-7322567-4-3 (ebook)

CIP information available upon request.

All rights reserved. The scanning, uploading, and electronic sharing of any part of this book without the permission of the publisher constitute unlawful piracy and theft of the author's intellectual property. If you would like to use material from the book (other than for review purposes), prior written permission must be obtained by contacting the publisher at info@blydynsquarebooks.com

Credits:

*Illustrations by Alyssa Beard*
*Cover design by Libby Juliano*
*Interior Layout by Kurt Weber*

"To Look at Any Thing" from THE LIVING SEED by John Moffitt. Copyright © 1961 by John Moffitt, renewed 1989 by Henry Moffitt. Reprinted by permission of Houghton Mifflin Harcourt Publishing Company. All rights reserved.

Quotes from *A River Runs Through It and Other Stories* by Norman Maclean, 1976, used with permission of University of Chicago Press; permission conveyed through Copyright Clearance Center, Inc.

"Three Little Birds," written by Bob Marley. Published by Fifty-Six Hope Road Music Limited/Primary Wave/Blue Mountain

*To look at any thing,*
*If you would know that thing,*
*You must look at it long:*
*To look at this green and say,*
*"I have seen spring in these*
*Woods," will not do—you must*
*Be the thing you see:*
*You must be the dark snakes of*
*Stems and ferny plumes of leaves,*
*You must enter in*
*To the small silences between*
*The leaves,*
*You must take your time*
*And touch the very peace*
*They issue from.*

—John Moffitt

# Acknowledgments

It takes a village to make a book. I would like to thank my little village of readers, editors, and supporters who helped me bring this book into being.

To Tara Tomczyk at Blydyn Square Books: Thank you for believing in this book, and for your always dead-on edits and comments that have made it so much stronger than that first draft you read many moons ago.

To my many readers, including Barbara Clark, Whitney (McKnight) Fishburn, Carolyn Levin, and Kathy Hoy, for your invaluable feedback.

To my partner Rachael Noble, for patiently listening as I read her parts of this book, and for being there every step of the way.

For Dr. B., for all you taught me.

For my siblings, for supporting me and my children through lots of ups and downs.

And most of all, for my parents, for never giving up on me, even when I wanted to give up on myself.

# Table of Contents

Author's Note . . . . . . . . . . . . . . . . . . . . . . . . . . . . . . . . . . 7

The Great Letting Go . . . . . . . . . . . . . . . . . . . . . . . . . . . 9

Taking Measure . . . . . . . . . . . . . . . . . . . . . . . . . . . . . . . 19

Riding the Leviathan . . . . . . . . . . . . . . . . . . . . . . . . . . 32

Valley of First Loves . . . . . . . . . . . . . . . . . . . . . . . . . . . 45

Doubts and Resolutions . . . . . . . . . . . . . . . . . . . . . . . . 60

River of the Spirit . . . . . . . . . . . . . . . . . . . . . . . . . . . . . 69

Brands and Bean Burritos . . . . . . . . . . . . . . . . . . . . . . 83

Bob Marley and Matters of the Mind . . . . . . . . . . . . . 105

Dr. B. and the School of the Self . . . . . . . . . . . . . . . . . 124

The Splinter of Discontent . . . . . . . . . . . . . . . . . . . . . 139

Mystic Pizza, Magic Oatmeal . . . . . . . . . . . . . . . . . . . 162

The Other Side of Faith . . . . . . . . . . . . . . . . . . . . . . . . 173

Resilience . . . . . . . . . . . . . . . . . . . . . . . . . . . . . . . . . . . 187

In the Company of Trees . . . . . . . . . . . . . . . . . . . . . . . 201

Rebellion of the Salt-Seeking Spirit . . . . . . . . . . . . . . 211

The Quarry . . . . . . . . . . . . . . . . . . . . . . . . . . . . . . . . . . 221

Coming Home . . . . . . . . . . . . . . . . . . . . . . . . . . . . . . . 232

Postscript: New Beginnings . . . . . . . . . . . . . . . . . . . . 237

References ................................... 244

Appendix: The Marketing Funnel .................... 245

Further Reading ................................ 247

About the Author ............................... 252

About the Illustrator ............................ 252

# Author's Note

The events described in this story happened a number of years ago. I've reconstructed them here as best as I remember them. Some of the locales mentioned may have changed since I made my long walk home. Certain people's names have also been changed for reasons of confidentiality and privacy. All information about the unnamed company referenced in this book is based on publicly available news reports in the *New York Times*, the *Wall Street Journal*, *Bloomberg*, and other reputable media outlets.

# 1

# The Great Letting Go

*When I let go of what I am, I become what I might be.*

—Lao Tzu

A few weeks before my fifty-sixth birthday, I was sitting in my office at the headquarters of the technology company where I had worked for twenty-eight years when I received the call that no one, especially at that age, wants to get.

It was the chief marketing officer, calling on his cell from wherever he was traveling that week.

"Bad news," he said. "Paul's restructuring."

Paul was the new CEO who had joined the company earlier in the year. Everyone in the firm had been on pins and needles for news of a downsizing, since that's what usually happened whenever a new CEO came onboard. As the company's head of communications, I was normally among the first to know about these things because my team would have to put together the plan for communicating the news to employees and spinning it to the media and investors.

"All right," I sighed, already searching through my computer files for the playbook we used for communicating corporate restructurings. "What do we need to do?"

"No, Jim," he replied. "This is about you."

I went quiet as he gave me the news. The new CEO was shaking up his management team and wanted to bring on a new head of communications. The good news, the chief marketing officer went on to say, was that the change wasn't happening right away. A search was underway for my replacement, which would probably take a couple of months. In the meantime, I was still in the job, but I would be advised to start looking around for something else, because my long run with this company was coming to an end.

"Wait," I said when I was able to find my voice. "I'm being let go? Why?"

"It's nothing personal. He's just looking for a different style of leader."

Nothing personal? What could be more personal than being let go from your job? I found myself protesting uselessly. This made no sense. I had a stellar reputation in the company. I had been getting excellent performance reviews for as long as I had been there and had just gotten another good one in the spring.

"Yeah, well," he replied, "there's a new sheriff in town and everything's different now."

After hanging up, I sat for a while in my office sorting through a churning blender of emotions. The month before, I had celebrated my one-year mark of completing chemotherapy for colon cancer. My scans were clean, and though I still had miles to go on my cancer journey, I was feeling like I had dodged a bullet with my name written on it.

And now this.

I had kids in college. A mortgage, medical bills, aging parents. Would I be able to find another job with a salary anywhere near what I was being paid? Would another company even be interested in me, considering my age and the fact that I had worked so long at one place? Would this precipitate another plunge into the hell of clinical depression? I had a long history of brushes with the black beast, but he and I had come to a détente and it had been more than a decade since we had wrestled in the pit together. The last thing I wanted to do was poke his sorry hide and get him riled up again.

So many questions, so many emotions. Fear. Anger. Disgust. Disbelief. I had given so much of my life to this company. I had always been a star performer and had a shelf full of awards to show for it. Now, suddenly, I was expendable? How could they be doing this to me?

At a certain level, having worked as long as I had in communications and investor relations, I knew the answer to my own question: This was about cutting costs. The company had been restructuring and downsizing from the day I first got there nearly twenty-eight years ago. What was then an IT giant with a hundred thousand employees and ten billion dollars in annual revenue was now down to less than a quarter of that size.

In my time with the firm, I had seen literally tens of thousands of people—entire cities—ushered out the door. But those reductions had always happened to other people.

Now my time had come. The restructurer's scythe had come for me.

As I sat in my office reeling from the news, my mind went back to another dark day a couple years earlier.

I had gone in for what I thought was a routine colonoscopy, my first after hitting the half-century mark. I had been putting it off because I was super busy and, well, who wants to have a colonoscopy? There was no history of colon cancer in my family. I wasn't overweight, had never smoked a cigarette in my life, and watched what I ate and worked out regularly. Why bother?

But at the urging of a colleague at work, I made the appointment and went in for the scope the Friday before Christmas. After I woke up from the procedure, the gastroenterologist took me into a private room and closed the door.

"It's a good thing you came in," he said gravely.

This was not what I was expecting. I was expecting to be handed a pack of peanut butter crackers and a bottle of grape juice and be sent on my way until my next roto-rooter in ten years. Instead, here was this bespectacled young doctor looking quite serious. They had found an overgrown polyp in my ascending colon, he informed me. The polyp was too big to be clipped off, but they had taken a snip for testing.

"We should have the results back within a week," he said, "but from the looks of it, I am quite confident it is cancerous."

The biopsy results the following week confirmed his suspicions of adenocarcinoma. They didn't know how advanced it was and wouldn't know until they did more tests. But I was going to need surgery to cut out the tumor, and maybe chemotherapy as well.

That shock of learning I had colon cancer had been existential in nature. It had woken me up to the reality of my own mortality in ways that all my past accidents, mishaps, depressions, and illnesses had not.

This latest news, of losing my job, was a cut of a different kind. It went to the core of who I was, or who I saw myself to be. I had worked for this company for half my life. I had been employed there for twice as long as I had been married to my ex-wife. For all of its faults and seemingly endless flows of red ink, this place was home. I was familiar with it, and it with me. There was something comforting in that familiarity: the people, the struggles, the shared history. Even this office. Sure, I didn't have a window view. But it was a damn nice office. All my things were here. Pictures of my boys and my parents. My awards. My books on the shelf. My files. Everything was where I knew it would be when I walked into the office in the morning.

Now that ground was being pulled out from beneath my feet and I felt like I was free falling. Who was I without this company? What was I? Where would I go, what would I do?

There are many awesome things about working for a big company: the pay, the benefits, the opportunities to work with really smart people and learn new skills and travel to cool places on someone else's dime. But do it for long enough, as I have, and you begin to feel like one of those tiny remora suckerfish that spend their entire lives riding the backs of sharks and whales. You're not sure who or what you are outside of this creature you're riding. Am I a fish or mammal? Is this the only view there is of the ocean? Why does everything around here taste like whale meat?

And when the leviathan you're riding is perpetually restructuring, life becomes an exhausting roller-coaster ride of near-death experiences. Every year, it seems, there's a new round of fat-trimming, except all the fat is long gone and the cuts are now going deep into the muscle. People you've worked with for years are no longer around, and the relief you feel for still having a job is mixed with heavy doses of survivor's guilt. *Hey, what happened to Joe? Jeez, why would they lay him off? He's the only one around here who knows how to do that job!*

The thing about big-company restructurings, at least the ones I've been through, is that though the people get downsized, the work does not. The processes remain in place; the customers still need to be served; the systems still need to be serviced and kept running. Invariably, all this work gets laid on the plates of the people who remain, who end up doing two or three jobs. Meanwhile, the executives at the top are always changing. It's like a turnstile up there. They stay for a few years, bring in their buddies, take their big bonuses, and then move on to the next gig, while the long-timers are left holding the bag. With all the changes at the top, you're never sure exactly what the strategy is or where the company is supposed to be going.

Do this for long enough and you develop a certain scab of skepticism about yet another restructuring aimed at doing what the last few had not. Maybe the new management team sensed that with me. I don't know. All I knew was that I had never been "let go" from any job before and I didn't know quite what to do, what to think.

Aware of a rising tide of panic within me, I got up and stepped out of my office onto the second floor.

This was before COVID-19, back in the days when people still congregated freely without masks and mandatory six-feet distancing orders at corporate offices across America, and on this day, the floor was bustling with activity. Doing my best to avoid eye contact with anyone lest I get pulled into an impromptu hallway meeting, I moved quickly to the side entrance.

It was a stunning mid-October afternoon: crisp and cool, sun shining overhead in a cloudless blue sky, trees ablaze in their fall colors. As soon as I got outside, I felt an immediate shift in my mood—lighter, clearer, able to separate myself a bit from the anxiety I was feeling and gain some perspective. Anxiety had been part of my journey for so long that I had come to accept her as an ugly but necessary companion in the carriage next to me and to do my best to keep her as comfortable as possible. Acceptance was one way to do that. Distraction was another. But the best way was to get outside into nature, which was why I spent as much time there as possible.

I took a few steps up the campus road. Every step farther away I got from the headquarters building, the lighter I felt. I began to be aware of another emotion rising within me amid the blender swirl of fear and anxiety and anger. I felt a palpable sense of relief, gratitude almost, as if I had been let out of jail. It had not been easy being at the company of late. Morale wasn't good and my health had been suffering. I was working nights and weekends, unable to take time off and spend quality time with my kids and my aging parents. I was having trouble sleeping. I had developed a searing pain in my neck that the doctors were at a loss to explain. At times the pain was so bad, I could barely sit at my desk.

I was fried. Used up. A cinder. Deep down, I didn't want to be at the company any longer, and the fact was, it was long since time for me to go. After all, who stays twenty-eight years at one company anymore? I had done well there, rising from a lowly editor of new product announcements to head of communications for a multibillion-dollar technology company. But now those opportunities had dried up. I had ridden this whale for as far as it could take me. It was time to move on.

I stood on the entrance road for a long while staring vacantly at the office building. I had spent more time in that building over the past three decades than I had at home. I had given this once-proud company the most productive years of my career. I had learned a lot, had a chance to work with some really great people, had some fun times. But it was just a job, just a building. It was not me and it was not my home.

I was aware of a raw, welling energy inside of me, a thrumming mix of terror and excitement, like a skydiver about to jump out of the plane. The leviathan had served me well, but I was not attached to it any longer. This remora fish had let go.

Turning away, I continued walking up the campus road away from the building. I walked past the lot where my car was parked. I walked by the copse of trees that I would pass on the drive home, where I often would see deer out grazing on warm summer evenings when I had to work late. I walked past a couple of other businesses at the end of the corporate campus, and when I came to the intersection, I turned right, in the direction of home.

And then I just kept walking.

# 2

# Taking Measure

*I have measured out my life with coffee spoons.*

—T. S. Eliot

About a mile into my walk, the thought struck me: *What are you doing, Jim? Home is more than twenty miles away. Do you plan to walk the whole way? It will take hours! This is nuts!*

Another voice within me, long dormant, answered back: *Exactly.*

It was crazy. It was irresponsible. But I didn't feel like being rational and responsible at that moment. I had been rational and responsible for a long time, and it had served me well in many ways in my life and my career. Now I wanted to do something out of the ordinary, at least within the context of what I had been doing for so long.

For twenty-eight years, I had been taking this route back and forth to the office, and like millions of other people in this great commuter nation, my purpose had been to travel the route as quickly as possible. Despite my literary bent, I have an analytical mind, and I went about my daily commute with the ruthless efficiency of Frederick Winslow Taylor applying the principles of scientific management to the factory floor. The shortest route between my house and the office was twenty-two miles. But the shortest route wasn't always the most efficient route time-wise, thanks to traffic, school bus routes, exasperatingly long red lights, and other factors.

And so I had studied maps and traffic patterns. I worked out primary routes and backup routes, so I knew where to go when I encountered an accident or traffic jam. I took pleasure in outsmarting traffic, speed limits, and slow drivers, all in the interest of beating the clock. The fastest time I ever clocked in my daily drive home from the office was thirty-six minutes, measured from the point I left the company parking lot to when I pulled into my garage at home.

The longest time—well, I never measured that, because it was wasted time, and my analytical mind did not do well with wasted time. I had so many other things I wanted and needed to be doing. I needed to mow the lawn before it got dark. I needed to stop at the grocery store so I had something to make dinner for my kids. I needed to visit my parents, which I hadn't had time to do because I'd been so busy with work. I needed to get down on paper this fantastic idea for a poem that had been eating at me for weeks but I'd not had time to write.

Efficiency, efficiency, efficiency. There were only so many hours in the day to get everything done—more precisely, there were twenty-four hours in a day and the job took half of them. Sleep consumed another seven or eight hours and my morning exercise routine took another hour, which, if I was lucky, left me with maybe a couple hours of available free time for all the other things I needed to do. The last thing I wanted to be doing with those precious free hours was sitting in my car stuck in traffic.

So I maneuvered. I dodged. I cut through side streets and parking lots. I ran stale (very stale) yellow lights. I raced demon-like through neighborhoods and shopping districts and highway bypasses with pedal to the metal and eyes straight ahead, seeing nothing but macadam and tail lights. The mind of a commuter is not focused on taking in the sights and scenes along the way. The goal is to traverse the distance between Point A and Point B as rapidly as possible without getting stopped for a speeding ticket, which obviously would be counterproductive to the whole efficiency cause.

That was me for the years I was riding the leviathan. Even as, in my personal life, I was studying practicing mindfulness and meditation to quiet my overactive mind and learn to be more in the present moment, I was, in my daily work, in a mad race against time, consumed with the goal of beating my best-ever commute time of thirty-six minutes from office parking lot to home garage. I never did beat that time, but if I did, my victory celebration would have been short-lived, because my new goal would have been to beat it again.

But now the race is over. I don't have to make the commute any longer. I'm done with it, or will be as soon as the company finds a new remora fish to take my place. The unconscious, foot-on-the-pedal, mad-demon routine of my life has been altered. The line has been broken. There's no more Point B, no more corporate office to drive to every day—at least not that office back there.

And now that I don't have to run that race any longer, what I want to do is take a nice long walk. I want to see—*really* see—the route that I have been unconsciously racing through for twenty-eight years, and maybe in the walking learn something about what I want to do for the next twenty-eight years, if I'm fortunate enough to have that many.

And if I don't learn anything—well, at least it's a really nice day for a walk.

## Walking Down Union Meeting

I am on a road called Union Meeting that runs straight as a proverbial arrow through a residential neighborhood of older stone homes. There are no sidewalks here, so I walk on the grass along the road's edge to stay out of the way of passing cars.

It being early afternoon on a weekday, there isn't a lot going on in the neighborhood. I see a couple of delivery men carrying boxes from an appliance truck toward the front door of one of the houses. I hear a leaf blower whining in the distance. I catch sight of a cute calico cat watching me from a front bay window. The houses are all colonials, probably fifty or sixty years old, generally well maintained except for one that is rundown with stuff strewn across the yard as if the owners didn't have enough room to keep it all inside. There's always at least one sore thumb in every neighborhood.

Likely when these homes were built, this was the development to be in. Over the years, it has transformed into a thoroughfare neighborhood that commuters like me speed through on their way to work. I find myself wondering about the people who live in these houses and what kind of lives they live. Doubtless they are a lot like me. Not being independently wealthy, they have to work for a living, and unless they are among the fortunate ones who are able to work from home, they're commuters, too. Just like mine, their days on this planet are characterized by a routine sameness. They get up at the same early hour to shower and dress and drive to work, and at the end of a long day at the office, they drive home to have dinner with their families and unwind for a couple of hours before going to bed. Five days of this and finally it's the weekend. Time to get chores done, take kids to sports games, maybe have friends over, and when Monday comes around, the cycle starts all over again.

A Henry David Thoreau quote comes to me from when I read *Walden* back in high school English class: "The mass of men lead lives of quiet desperation."

Do the people in these homes lead lives of quiet desperation? Are they stressed out from too many demands and responsibilities and not enough time for themselves? Do they have unfulfilled dreams that eat at them like acid as they go about the daily drudgery of serving their employers and taking care of their obligations? Do they secretly wish for something else for their lives but are unsure how to make it happen?

I can't say. For all I know, the people in these homes are blissfully happy. I can only say that the mass of working men and women I've known over the years have not seemed very happy. They complained, often bitterly, about senior leaders who were earning ten times what they themselves were making but didn't have the time to stop by their offices to say hello or thank them for their contributions. They resented managers who didn't communicate very well, who didn't ask for their opinions before making decisions that affected their work and their personal lives. They felt micromanaged by people who were less knowledgeable than they were and pigeonholed in roles that weren't taking full advantage of their talents and gifts.

In hallways, in offices, in cafeterias and at water-coolers, I would hear these people talk wistfully of other things they would rather be doing, if only they had the courage and the means to do so. They had dreams of opening up a yoga studio, a wood-working shop, a graphic-design business. This dog-eat-dog corporate environment really didn't suit them—they really, really wanted to get the hell out and be their own bosses—but the job paid so darn well, and they had bills to pay, families to take care of. They liked being able to count on that steady paycheck every week. And so they stayed, even though they didn't love it. They came to work every day to take their designated place on the whale's back and feed upon its rich and succulent flesh, all the while longing to be doing something, anything, other than what they were doing.

Studies[1] back this up. Gallup's World Poll showed that only 15 percent of the world's workers feel engaged at work, and that many people hate their jobs and particularly their bosses. Time will tell whether the COVID-19 pandemic has altered those stats in any meaningful way, but the reality is that the majority of American workers are not feeling particularly happy and fulfilled in their jobs.

## A Life of Quiet Desperation

As for me, well, I can say with absolute certainty that I had been leading a life of quiet desperation for many of the years I had worked for the company. Yes, there had been many good times, many exciting and fulfilling times, times when I was learning new things and being promoted and made to feel valued and important by the people I worked with. The money, too, I admit, was satisfying, if only in a temporal way. There is something deeply gratifying to the ego to be paid well for the work you do. A paycheck is immediate recognition of one's value to the world, and who doesn't want that?

But all the money and ego gratification in the world will ring hollow if the heart isn't in the work, and mine often wasn't. As successful as I was in my time with the company, it was never really what I wanted to be doing. Even as I was going to photo shoots in Budapest and Tokyo, flying in a helicopter over the Statue of Liberty to investor meetings in New York City, managing people and agencies around the world—even as the firm was giving me opportunities and experiences I likely would never have enjoyed on my own—I longed to be sitting in a mountain cabin in my jeans writing the great American novel or a book of plain-verse poetry in the style of Robert Frost.

To be an author: That was my dream. I knew it from the time I was a teenager, when I would sit up in my second-floor bedroom of our old farmhouse and fill notebook upon notebook with stories and poems and anything else that came to me. If you had asked me back then what I wanted to do for the rest of my life, working in the corporate world would have been last on my list. Like Thoreau, I saw corporations as greedy, spirit-sucking machines that made people into automatons. Corporations were where souls went to die, and I was determined not to let it happen to me.

But I did, I think, as I walk down the road on this lovely October afternoon.

I did let it happen. I've spent the past twenty-eight years spinning news and creating PowerPoint decks and putting lipstick on often lousy financial results.

I'm a PR pitchman. A reluctant spokesperson. I've used my talents, such as they are, in service of a struggling leviathan that is now tossing me off its back, and if my soul wasn't dead, it was on life support.

How did I get so far away from my dreams?

## How Did I Get Here?

When I joined the company at the age of twenty-seven after a stint in journalism, I knew nothing of the corporate world except that it paid a lot better than the newspaper job I'd been working. I had just completed an MFA in creative writing and was working on a novel. My plan was to work for a few years and save up my money while finishing up the novel in my spare time, then move to New York City and launch my career as an author.

But life had other plans. The novel wasn't any good and never found a publisher. Meanwhile, I got married; bought a house; had the first of my three sons, followed shortly thereafter by the other two. Suddenly, I had big responsibilities—and the bills that come along with them.

At the same time, I was finding, to my surprise, that I was actually pretty good at this corporate stuff. Yeah, it wasn't really what I wanted to be doing, but the pay was good and the company was promoting me and giving me opportunities to advance and make more money.

So I stayed. Five years became ten. I got a big promotion to director of investor relations and was now representing the company to Wall Street financial analysts and investment houses. This was during the dotcom boom when stocks were soaring and the world was partying because, well, it was 1999. I knew nothing of this world of sell-side analysts and hedge funds—I was an English major in college, for God's sake—and so I went back to school at night for an MBA.

It was all very exciting. Between work and night school and stuff with the boys, I was busier than ever. I still wrote on the side when I had time, still dreamed of one day becoming a published writer. But how could I leave the company now? In addition to a six-figure salary, I was being granted stock options and performance grants. Every promotion, every equity grant, every perk was locking me ever tighter onto the body of the great provider whale.

Ten years became fifteen. Fifteen years became twenty. Somewhere in this time, I went through a devastating divorce and took on the equivalent of a jumbo mortgage payment every month in alimony and child support. Meanwhile, the world's financial system was crashing and my savings and 401k had dwindled to next to nothing.

So I worked even harder, put in even longer hours. I was at my desk by seven o'clock in the morning to faithfully serve my employer, which needed my help more than ever. The Great Recession was doing a number on the business and the company was restructuring and downsizing once again. With every slice of flank taken off, I was given opportunities to take on more responsibility. By my twenty-fifth year there, I was running the global communications function, bringing home multiples of what I had been making when I started there.

## The Pursuit of Growth

Would I have been happier at another company, I wonder as I walk, a company that was better managed and more successful? Maybe, at least somewhat. Everyone wants to work for a winner, after all. The rewards are always greater for a growing organization. Shrinking companies never have enough money or resources to spread around. Opportunities for movement are more limited. In the words of a former boss of mine, the organization becomes constipated.

But whether fabulously successful or bleeding red ink, in the end all corporations come from the same mold. They may have different sizes and shapes and logo colors, but they are all complex, slow-moving beasts with huge appetites whose objective is to grow as big and profitable as possible, because that is what their shareholders demand of them. A whale that is not growing is dead meat to Wall Street and will quickly be fed to the sharks of corporate raiders and turnaround specialists. Conversely, a firm that is steadily growing its revenue, margins, profits, cash flow, and market share will be rewarded with rich multiples in its stock price, which can then be used to gobble up smaller fish in the ocean, thereby continuing the virtuous cycle of growth.

Growth is music to the ears of investors, but it comes at the cost of anonymity and depersonalization. The bigger the mammal grows, the more resources it requires to keep all its internal machinery going. The bigger it grows, the less the people at the head of the whale know, or can know, about the individual lives and circumstances of the thousands of remora fish that ride its flesh through the blue waters of the marketplace. All big corporations will tell you that this is not the case, that they know and care about their people. But the reality is, they're too busy consuming to care about anything other than how to sustain their ever-growing heft. They are in a battle for finite resources and finite growth in a finite market, and that means swallowing anything that gets in their way.

For a real whale, growth is sustained by eating lots of plankton and krill, until it reaches the end of its lifespan, turns belly up, and becomes carrion for other creatures on the food chain. For corporate leviathans, growth is created and sustained through decidedly unnatural means. It comes with policies and processes. It comes with procedures and paperwork. It comes with titles and job levels and pay schemes.

It also comes with politics—a lot of politics. All of the less admirable traits that go with being human—arrogance, greed, selfishness, jealousy, unbridled ambition, small-mindedness, rumor-mongering—get magnified in a corporate setting. Work in a corporate environment for nearly thirty years as I have and you will see enough political maneuvering and backstabbing to kill your faith in humanity. You will see less capable people in higher positions for the simple reason that they are good at selling themselves to the executive suite. You will see people without an ounce of creativity taking credit for your ideas and hard work. You will be given plans to execute that make no sense but you have to do them because a higher-up says so. You will be thrown under the bus when those plans fail, as they inevitably do, and you will want to scream or cry or both at the same time.

## Playing the Game

To do well in this artificial corporate world, you have to be a certain kind of animal. You have to accept and buy into the fact that success is not just about intelligence and capability and doing a great job. It's also about playing the game. You have to be good at working the system for your own personal advancement and benefit. You need to be willing to step on people to move up that next rung on the ladder. You have to be good at selling yourself, not just to those above you, but to recruiters, headhunters, board members, and anyone else involved in getting to that next rung on the ladder.

If you want to rise to the very top positions of power in a big company, you have to enjoy playing this game. It has to be something that fires you up in the morning. You have to enjoy putting on a mask every day and pretending to be someone you're not in order to gain leverage and influence. You have to like rubbing noses with people in power and finding ways to get them to like you and give you what you want. When those people in power do or say something you don't agree with, you have to be able to hold yourself back from speaking the truth, so as not to break glass and bruise often fragile egos.

For me, though, and for a lot of the people I've worked with, this is all a very unnatural act. We just don't fit into this corporate environment. We don't want to stroke egos and play politics. We just want to do our jobs well and get paid fairly for it. As lucrative as the corporate game can be, there's something fake about the whole thing. You can never really be totally yourself for fear of revealing something that doesn't conform to the polished image that the company wants to present to the world.

And for God's sake, don't mention to anyone in the office that you're having problems at home and maybe struggling with anxiety and depression. That's a sure career killer. Word will get up to the executive suite and you'll never get promoted. There is no place for weakness in these waters.

Play this game day after day, year after year, decade after decade, and it can leave you empty. It's exhausting having to wear all those masks and maintain some kind of consistency among them. You just want to throw it all off like a set of ill-fitting clothes and go sit in the woods for a few weeks until your head clears out and you can think again.

# 3

# Riding the Leviathan

*Night and day, wind and storm, tide and earthquake, impeded man no longer. He had harnessed Leviathan. All the old literature, with its praise of Nature, and its fear of Nature, rang false as the prattle of a child.*

—E. M. Forster

So, *why did you do it then, Jim?* I ask myself as I continue walking down Union Meeting Road, past comfortable suburban colonial homes. Why did you stay as long as you did in this *corporate world if it didn't fit you well and it wasn't what you really wanted to be doing?*

The answer comes back quickly: *It was security. I stayed for the security.*

The advantage of riding a corporate leviathan is that there is plenty to feed on, even when the beast is shedding people and divisions. The pockets of fat are deep, and if you are good at what you do and you solve problems for people higher up than you, you will be promoted and paid handsomely. Indeed, you will be paid multiples of what the average person in this world could ever hope to earn. You will be paid so much that you lose perspective on what you actually need to live a secure, happy life on this planet. You begin to think your worth as an individual is somehow tied to the title you hold and the salary you bring home. You think you and your loved ones won't be able to get by if you don't continue bringing home that big salary, even as you live in a house ten times the size of what you really need and pay more in taxes than the average worker makes in a year.

A certain fear begins to creep in. You begin to think you *need* to remain attached to this slow-moving, herring-gobbling beast to survive in the shark-infested waters. It is your benefactor, your protector. You like the feeling of being attached to something of size and substance. After all, a corporation displaces a lot of water as it lumbers through the marketplace. It can't easily be swallowed or brought down. It commands respect and awe. It can bust through barriers that smaller creatures can't. It can take advantage of its economies of scale to offer its employees all kinds of perks and benefits they can't get on their own.

Not everyone wants these things, of course. There is a breed of risk-takers and entrepreneurs who prefer to make their own way through the open seas rather than riding on the back of a big company. They enjoy the thrill of starting their own businesses or working for small startups with only an idea and barely enough capital to make payroll.

But that's not me or most people I know. Most people want to know where that next paycheck will be coming from. Is it any surprise, then, that in the wake of the Great Recession of 2008–2009 and the Great Lockdown of 2020, more Americans than ever before are working for large companies?[2] They want the certainty that comes from knowing they are standing on something big and solid.

## A Devil's-Pact Trade

But this certainty comes at a cost. There's a huge price to be paid in terms of your personal freedom and potential. When you are hooked to the flesh of a big company, you do what it needs you to do. You go where it tells you to go. You learn what it needs you to learn, not necessarily the other way around. The arc of your career and life is circumscribed by the trajectory of the company itself. You never truly know how high or far you can go on your own because you only need to go as high and as far as the organization needs you to. When it tells you to move your family to another state, you pack your bags and go. When it needs your help on nights and weekends and vacations, you do it. When it has an itch, you scratch it—and there are a lot of itches to attend to when you work for a large organization. They've given you a big swath of skin to take care of, after all. There used to be three people doing this work, but the other two guys got laid off as part of an efficiency drive to add another nickel to earnings per share. It's only you now, and if you don't scratch the itch, they'll find someone else who can. There are plenty of remora fish in the sea.

So you do it. You put in twelve-hour days, sacrifice nights and weekends and vacation time with your family, all to maintain the standard of living you feel is necessary for you to be secure—and for every minute you are chained to your desk staring into the crystal screen of your LCD monitor, you are losing out on the most precious asset that you have in your life: time.

Time to do things you want to do.

Time to spend with your spouse and kids.

Time to sit with your aging parents and hear their life stories.

Time to travel and take adventures to places you've never been.

Time to garden and fish and go for a hike.

Time to read books and write poetry.

Time to pursue your passions, your interests, your gifts.

This is a big one. Maybe, like me, you feel you have a calling, a greater purpose on this planet. Every day, a voice nags at you: *Pay attention to me! Pay attention to me!* But you push it away because, well, you've got to pay the bills. Dreams do not pay bills. Dreams are things that children have, and you're an adult now. You have responsibilities.

You recognize at some level that this is what you're doing, that you've made a kind of devil's-pact trade of passion for security, though you're not particularly happy about it. Deep inside, frustration burns. You begin to resent the company and the people who run it for the demands they make on you. You want your time back, your life back. You want so much just to let go of your place on the beast's itch-infested back and be free again. The urge is so strong, you can taste it. You dream of it. You dream about how good it would feel to be swimming free through the ocean waters, to be able to go where you want to go, do what you want to do, turning pirouettes in the water, whatever. You know how that feels because you were free once before, when you were young and life was as easy as the day is long.

## The Fear of Letting Go

But you don't do it. Though you feel disconnected from your life and your dreams, though your spouse and kids feel neglected, though you can't find the time to get to the things that need to be done at home, though your neck is killing you because of the stress—despite all this, you keep riding the company, allowing it to run your life, to own you.

Why?

For the money, of course. Or rather, for the feeling of security that money gives you, the feeling of standing on something solid and certain. To let go would be too risky.

Okay, okay, so years ago you dreamed of starting your own business. You had what you thought was a really good idea. Sometimes even today you think about that idea, that dream. But let's be real: You don't have what it takes to do something like that. That's something that people a lot smarter and bolder than you do. What happens if you jump ship (jump leviathan?) to do your own gig and things don't work out? What then? You may not ever get another big-company job, may never again be able to make the kind of money you were making before. How would you put food on the table for your family? What about college for your kids? What about medical insurance? You could get sick. Jeez, you could end up like those homeless people in New York City who sit on the street corner with a sign on their chest and a cup in their hand.

No, it's too risky. You've seen the commercials on TV and your smartphone newsfeed reminding you what a scary ocean it is out there. Sharks circling everywhere—sharks and illnesses and dread viruses and out-of-hand medical costs and soaring college tuitions and Social Security going away and robots taking whatever well-paying jobs aren't heading overseas. Best to stay right where you are, safely tethered to the back of the whale, riding it for all it's got, even as you inwardly seethe against the chains that bind you. It won't be for forever. You have a plan, a plan for freedom. The plan is to keep contributing to that corporate 401(k) plan, taking advantage of the company match and the power of compounding, until you have enough saved that you don't need the leviathan anymore.

And maybe you're lucky enough to do this until you turn sixty-five, and your health is still good, and you can make the leap to the safety net of Social Security and Medicare and perhaps a pension, too, to enjoy the golden years that you've spent your life working for.

Or maybe, like me, things are going along according to plan until one day the company decides it has too many sucker-fish tethered to its flesh. It announces a restructuring—a *workforce rebalancing*, as it's often euphemistically referred to in corporate America—and with a fling of its massive tail, you are released into the blue waters of the great big ocean, and you realize you haven't been standing on solid ground at all: It's just the broad back of a huge fish-mammal, and it's been so long since you've used your long-dormant fins that you fear you won't be able to swim on your own, and suddenly every little fish that comes at you looks like a shark.

## A Year Lost in Traffic

All of this comes to me with newfound clarity as I walk along the road, unshackled from the company for the first time in twenty-eight years. This is what I've been doing, I realize. I have been giving over my most finite and precious asset—time—in return for a feeling of security that in reality was nothing but an illusion.

And that's just the time I was dutifully working in my office. What about all the time I spent commuting back and forth to the office? That truly was lost time.

I do some mental calculations and figure that over the course of my twenty-eight years working there, I spent about ten thousand hours in my car. Ten thousand hours! That's more than a year of my life stuck in traffic. Jeez, what could I have done with that year? I could have written a book. I could have traveled the world. I could have learned carpentry and done volunteer work for Habitat for Humanity.

And my daily commute of forty-five minutes isn't all that bad compared to what many other people go through. I know people who commute an hour and a half to work each day—one way! Studies show that before COVID-19 hit, commute times for the average American had been getting longer and longer.[3] We've been spending more of our precious days in our car out to beat the clock. But there is no beating the clock—that's the thing. The clock is the clock. The clock is fixed, and there's nothing we can do to make it shorter or longer than it is. Sixty seconds per minute. Sixty minutes per hour. Twenty-four hours in the day, three hundred sixty-five days in the year.

And how many years? That's the big question. How many years of life do we get? That's a fixed number, too, though none of us knows what our number is. Who wants to spend their precious years fighting lights and traffic and twelve-wheel trucks that think they're race cars?

Not me or anyone else I know. But we have to do it, because the bills need to be paid. Which is why, I think, so many of us have this love-hate relationship with our big-company employers. We love the money and the benefits and the feeling of security all of this brings to us and our families. But we hate the feeling of being owned, on the clock, our time not our own.

## Thoreau's Experiment in the Woods

Is this, I wonder, what Henry David Thoreau meant by the mass of men leading lives of quiet desperation? When he wrote those words, Thoreau was living in a tiny cabin in the Massachusetts woods by the shores of his beloved Walden Pond, where he had gone to escape the jaws of encroaching industrialization. This was in the mid-1800s, at the dawn of large corporations. The leviathans of his day were railroad and telegraph companies offering more efficient alternatives to the horse for moving people, goods, and information across great distances.

Many people back then were praising the great progress being made by the machine of industrialism. Thoreau wasn't so sure. Being a fierce individualist and lover of nature, he did not like what he was seeing as people trudged off to work every day to toil away for monolithic organizations that were profiting off the backs of the natural world. Trains were loud and they spewed clouds of steam and they ran on ugly rails that cut through pristine fields and valleys. And what about the toll on the people who worked for them? Thoreau saw that toll in the faces of the townspeople in nearby Concord. They looked tired, joyless, spiritless. "We do not ride on the railroad," he wrote in *Walden*. "It rides upon us."

The corporations of today are of a different stripe. They are technology companies, oil refiners, health-care providers, media conglomerates, search and social networking companies. But their goal is no different from the first railroad and telegraph conglomerates: to wring an ever-increasing amount of output and profits from a finite amount of capital.

Capital is the food that feeds the leviathan, and there are many different types of it. There's financial capital, such as bank loans, bond sales, and issuance of stock. There's the physical capital of raw materials and natural resources. There is manufactured or produced capital, such as finished goods or software. And then there is human capital, which is us—we employees who ride the whale's back and do its work.

All are part of the capital equation. All are swallowed up and processed in the belly of the beast to provide the energy it needs to survive and grow.

There is nothing wrong with this, of course. It is the beauty of the market-based capitalist system. But what feeds the beast does not necessarily feed the soul. Human capital is of an entirely different order from other forms of capital. Financial, physical, and manufactured capital can be stretched and squeezed and pushed to ever-greater levels of speed and productivity. It can be made to work 24/7, if need be, in service of the organization. Human beings cannot, because we are made of flesh and blood. We are complex, living creatures with needs of our own. We get tired. We have desires and longings beyond those that can be satisfied by our corporate provider.

Which is why, I think, so many people I know in the corporate world are burned out. We are human inputs in a relentless inhuman efficiency machine that demands of us ever-greater amounts of productivity in order to meet the demands of its shareholders—all of which leaves us with scarce time and energy to attend to the things that feed our human souls.

## Playing It Safe

And then something else comes to me with newfound clarity as I make my way down Union Meeting Road.

No one made me do any of this.

No one forced me to make a devil's bargain of trading precious time for perceived security.

No one forced me to put on the shackles of working for a big company, and no one has prevented me from taking them off.

It's not the company's fault. It's not the system's fault. It's not the world's fault.

It was me. It was entirely my choice, from the day I accepted the offer from the company and decided to jump into this crazy corporate world. Every day I got in my car in the morning and made the race to the office, I was making a choice. And at the root of that choice was fear.

Fear, fear, fear. How much of our lives do we waste living in fear? I've done it, for sure. I think of all the fears that have kept me bound and shackled over the years. Fear of not having enough. Fear of not being good enough. Fear of failing. Fear of being rejected. Fear of not measuring up to my own standards. Fear of falling back down into that awful place where everything feels dark and hopeless.

It's all wasted energy. All wasted life.

Why did I stay at this company for so long? I stayed because, despite all my skills and capabilities and successes, deep down I did not fully believe in myself. I didn't believe in my ability to achieve my dreams and make a living from them. Meanwhile, the company kept promoting me, throwing more responsibility my way, taking me another rung up the ladder. I knew the job and could do it. It was a known quantity. Safer just to stay than to jump ship to somewhere else where I might fail.

Riding the back of a big company can be a way of hiding from yourself. There's safety in anonymity. You know that paycheck is going to be there every week, whereas you don't know whether this dream you've been harboring since you've been a kid is just that: a kid's fantasy. The way of the whale is a lot more certain than taking a chance on yourself.

And it wasn't just in my career that I chose safety, I realize. I chose safety in many other areas of my life as well.

Like not allowing myself to get into a serious relationship after my divorce because I was afraid of being burned again.

Like not submitting my writing to publishers and journals for fear that my stuff wasn't good enough.

Like not speaking in public for fear I would make a fool of myself.

Like not building my dream mountain house for fear that I would overextend myself financially, when in truth the money has always been there for me and my kids through every step of the way back from my divorce.

All of these things show a basic lack of faith in myself, in God, in the universe. I have, I realized, been playing it safe. And playing it safe isn't going to get me to my dreams.

***

A car whooshes by a yard to my left, going too fast, startling me out of my thoughts.

I picture the guy behind the wheel, driving unconsciously as I did for so many years, and I think, *Hey, slow down, buddy! What's the rush? It's a beautiful day!*

But he continues on, of course. As I would have done. As I no longer need to do now that the company is tossing me off its back. I feel oddly sorry for him as I continue walking on my solitary journey home.

# 4

# Valley of First Loves

*I never saw so sweet a face*
*As that I stood before.*
*My heart has left its dwelling-place*
*And can return no more.*

—John Clare

A mile and a half down the road, Union Meeting comes to a dead-end at an interstate road, where I have a choice.

I can turn left and make my way onto the always-busy Route 202, which I'm going to have to get onto at some point in order to get home. But I don't particularly relish the prospect of walking along a highway next to speeding cars spewing exhaust.

Or I can turn right in the direction of a back road that runs parallel to the highway. The back route has the advantage of being more scenic and avoiding some of the congestion. The downside is that it goes past a school bus depot, which on school days can be deadly to an efficient commute. But experience has taught me that as long as I stay away from certain windows of time in the early morning and mid-afternoon when the buses are out, the back route can be just as efficient time-wise as the highway, while a lot less rattling to the nerves.

I head right.

## A Dogleg onto School Road

Crossing over the interstate, I walk up a hundred yards and make a dogleg left onto School Road, presumably named after the old schoolhouse building on the corner. The school is now a historical society, but the lot behind it is being used by the district for the bus depot. Behind the depot gate I see a field of yellow school buses, row upon row of them lined up like a tank battalion ready to move out for battle. In another couple of hours, this depot will be teeming with action as drivers arrive to claim their numbered buses and head out on their afternoon routes.

I think of all the times in the past when I got caught behind a bus on my commute to work. There's nothing more maddening to an impatient, minute-counting commuter like me than getting caught behind a school bus. There you are, trying to set a new record commute time home, and suddenly you're behind a big old bus that's moseying down the road, doodle-doodle-doo, and then those dreaded blinking lights go on and the crossing arm comes out and you're stuck. There's nothing you can do. You can't turn around and you can't go forward; you have to just sit there watching a bunch of slow-poke schoolkids make their way out of the bus and spill onto the road, gabbing and waving breezily to the driver. Finally, they're out of the way, the lights go off, the crossing arm goes back, you heave a sigh of relief as the bus lumbers on, but then a hundred yards farther ahead, the lights flash again and you have to sit through another round of kid-discharging, until blessedly the bus turns into a development and you can make progress again. It's enough to make a person begin to hate the color yellow.

Beyond the depot, School Road is hemmed in on both sides by tall hedges, and I have to do some maneuvering to find enough road edge to walk. But after a mile or so, the hedges give way to the rolling green fairways of the Bluestone Country Club. Being that it's an unseasonably warm afternoon for mid-October, the course is crawling with golfers getting a round in before colder weather arrives. I see carts moving and flags waving and guys in shorts strolling the fairways. Nearby, a nattily dressed guy in a yellow polo shirt readies to tee off on the eleventh hole. His club swings back, there is a solid crack, and the ball rockets upward until I can't see it any longer. Nice hit, buddy!

I used to be a golfer back in high school but got away from it over the years. Though I enjoy golfing and often think how nice it would be to get out on the links, I am rarely able to carve out the time for it. Work sucks up every waking hour during the week, and weekends are for writing and kids' stuff and getting things done around the house. Golf is not a cheap hobby, either, and I have other things I'd rather spend my money on.

Career-wise, however, giving up my golf game probably wasn't a wise thing to do. Golf, after all, is more than just a sport. It's an extension of the workplace. It's where deals are done and relationships are forged. If you want to get to know people in positions of power and influence in corporate America, you had better have a membership at the country clubs where those people belong.

I don't believe I'm being cynical in saying this. I'm merely pointing out the reality of corporate America. If you want to win in the game of business, you need to play the game of golf, and I chose not to, just as I chose not to play the game of coddling headhunters and hopping like a cricket from job to job toting my family across the country in an endless hunt for more lucrative pastures. All of these things are smart things to do, professionally speaking. They are things that ambitious people do to advance their careers and make their way to the rarefied air at the top of the corporate ladder.

For me, though, with my warped way of looking at the world, these things just never felt natural or genuine. For whatever reason, I tend to run in the opposite direction from anything that smells of privilege and exclusivity. If I'm going to play a round of golf, it's because I want to be outside on a nice day enjoying the fresh air, not schmoozing with a bunch of senior execs with whom I always need to be on, on, on. I wear a mask every day at the office. Why would I want to put on another one when I venture out onto the links? I'd rather be out on a stream, where the only creature I'm trying to fool is a wary trout with a dry fly that I've tied myself from hackle and feathers.

Of course, there's a price to pay for this kind of foolish thinking. It's why I now find myself at the age of fifty-five about to be cut loose from my well-paying corporate job without a rolodex of headhunters to call to the rescue. This is something that those guys out on the links today totally get. To be part of the club, you have to pay your dues.

*You better get with it, Jim*, I admonish myself. *You're going to be out of a job soon. You need to get yourself out there more. Join a country club. Put away your precious ideals.*

I know it. I know all this in my head.

But I know I won't do it. I'm too stuck in my ways.

## Into the Enchanted Valley of Gwynedd

Pondering these thoughts, I leave behind the manicured greens of the country club and follow the road down into the lush wilds of Gwynedd Valley.

This is an enchanted area of deep woods and trickling creeks and old stone mills. The valley was settled in the 1600s by Welsh Quakers, who came here seeking haven to practice their peace-loving religious beliefs. This valley has always had a bit of a mystical feel to me, likely owing to its Welsh name and the many stone mansions that crown its hills, and also because it was here, in one of these old houses, where the first romantic love of my young life lived.

I say *love*, although knowing what I now know of love, I can say with certainty that what I was feeling back then was nothing but an infatuation whipped up by my seventeen-year-old body's raging hormonal system. That infatuation was directed at a girl in my high school class by the name of Caitlin, a name that spoke to me of everything that was exotic and pure about the opposite sex. She was dark and pretty with long silky hair and the face of an angel, along with a pair of lean, shapely legs that I couldn't keep my eyes off whenever I saw her wandering the halls of our little Catholic high school.

Being that she was uncommonly pretty—and also, by the way, popular and a star athlete—being that she was all these things wrapped up in one luscious package, all the boys in that school were after her. And being that I was not popular or all that athletic, Caitlin was not going to go for me, especially given my tendency to unravel into a mumbling mess whenever I tried to have a conversation with her. Steely self-confidence is every bit as important to winning over a girl as it is to being successful in the business world, and I had none of it at the time. My fumbling attempts to speak with Caitlin while she stood by her locker must have been as painful for her as they were for me. With my heart thrumming in my throat, I don't think I was able to communicate anything intelligible to her other than the fact that this boy was definitely not ready for the dating game.

At our many class parties during senior year, I would wander from room to room looking for Caitlin, hoping to catch a moment alone with her and maybe ask her out. It was all a fantasy, of course. I had no chance with her. I could only look helplessly on as she chatted with more popular boys by her locker in the school hallway. I knew that if I were ever going to be with Caitlin, I would need to break through my shyness and actually ask her out on a date. That's what other guys did, after all. But the thought of it was more daunting to me than having to take the SATs. Exams and schoolwork I could handle. This romance stuff I could not. I didn't seem to be equipped for it. Even thinking about asking Caitlin out on a date turned my insides into a fishbowl of darting minnows.

## The Gift and Curse of Sensitivity

These damn nerves of mine. They foiled me constantly. From the time I was little, I was aware of the propensity of my nervous system to overreact to things. My earliest memory was as a four-year-old, watching in panic through the living-room window as my mother walked out to the curb to the mailbox. She was only getting the mail, but I didn't know that. I thought she was leaving and never coming back. My heart raced; I couldn't breathe; I felt I was going to die.

Then she was back inside the house and everything was fine again. I hadn't died. I went back to my toys.

People said I was shy. A homebody. Excitable. I ate fast, talked fast, ran fast—propelled by an inner whorl of energy that rested only when I lay my head down on the pillow at night. I was constantly tripping, falling, breaking teeth and bones. I was super sensitive to criticism and would dwell on perceived slights for days. I hated having attention brought on myself. Ask me a question in class, or call me in front of the room to make a presentation, and it would unleash an army of angry demons within me. Today, I probably would be labeled with ADHD or an anxiety disorder and given pills.

But back then, aside from the accidents, there was no particular reason for my parents or teachers to be worried. I was happy. I did well in school. I was just being a boy.

But as the years went on, I began to be aware that something was different about me, and it had to do with how deeply I felt things. I could sense unspoken tension in a room. Conflict and arguments of any kind would set off alarm bells within me. I felt deeply other people's emotional upsets, especially my mother's. I could sense it when she was sad, when she was overwhelmed, when she was worried about money or issues with us kids.

My siblings weren't like this. Other kids I knew weren't like this. At least, they didn't seem to be. I felt as if I were walking around life with an extra antenna, picking up emotions wherever I went. I would hear a plaintive song on the radio, or the wash of the wind in a storm, or the patter of rain against the window, and a sudden rush of elation would course through me, raising goosebumps across my body. Joy and sorrow; happiness and sadness; highs and lows: They would rise unbidden within me like the tide, leaving me quivering in their wake.

It would take me another thirty years to realize that I was one of the fifteen percent or so of the population who are cursed—or blessed, depending on how you look at it—to be born highly sensitive people—aka HSPs. Back then, all I knew is that there was an emotional switch inside me that was easily triggered and I seemed to have no control over it. All I could do was go along for the ride.

By the time I got to high school, I knew my inner machinery well enough not to trust it, especially when it came to the risky realm of girls. What would happen if I went up to Caitlin to ask her out and she said no—or, even worse, laughed in my face? *You want to go out with a hot, popular chick like me?* The rejection would be calamitous. A fate worse than death.

But it really was do or die at this point. We were seniors now—high school was slipping away. Word was, Caitlin was planning to go away to college. Daily, I pondered how to go about asking this girl on a date. Daily, I failed.

## The Goodbye Girl

Graduation day came and went, and I no longer saw Caitlin in the school hallway. In the fall, she went away to college while I was still at home, commuting back and forth to classes at a local university campus. I wrote her a letter once (yes, back then, we handwrote letters and sent them through the mail) and I got a letter back from her, relating her experiences at school. I read and re-read that letter as if it were from the Pope, poring over each word, wondering what she was thinking as she wrote it. She had to know at this point that I was interested in her, that I wanted to go beyond the casual acquaintanceship that we had in high school.

She told me in the letter that she was coming home for the Christmas break. I determined I was going to take the opportunity to finally ask her out. When the holiday came around, I found her home phone number in the phonebook (yes, we still had physical phonebooks back in those days) and went up into my parents' bedroom to make the call. How my heart hammered in my chest as I dialed the number and heard Caitlin's voice on the other end of the line. I had my speech prepared but my mind was suddenly blank as Locke's tabula rasa.

At last I managed to find words. There was this new movie out, *The Goodbye Girl*. It looked pretty good, would she be interested in seeing it?

"Wait," she said, stopping my rambling. "Who is this?"

Jeez, I'd forgotten to tell her who was calling. What an idiot!

"Jim," I said. "Jim Kerr. You remember—from high school."

She giggled. "Yes, I remember you."

There was an awkward silence. Did I need to ask her again about the movie? I wasn't sure I had enough beats left in my heart to go through the whole spiel all over again.

"Have you seen it?" I managed to ask.

"Seen what?"

"*The Goodbye Girl*. With Richard Dreyfus."

She giggled again. I heard muffled sounds in the background—likely her family having a good laugh in the kitchen about Caitlin's phone call with a nervous suitor. "No. It sounds kind of sad . . ."

"I don't think it's sad," I came back quickly.

"When were you thinking?"

"Maybe next week?"

"Next week is Christmas."

"The week after? New Year's week?"

Another pause. More muffled sounds in the background. "Maybe. I got to check," she said. "My family has a bunch of parties. How about I get back to you? What's your number?"

I gave her the number and hung up, exhausted. But I had done it. I'd asked Caitlin out. Now it was just a matter of waiting for her to call back.

Christmas came and went and I didn't hear from her. But everyone was busy around Christmas. I would hear from her soon, I was sure.

More days passed. I was working at an appliance store over the break and every day I would come home from the store expecting there to be a note from my mother on the table: *A girl named Caitlin called. Said to call her back tonight. She'll be home.*

Every day there was no note waiting for me. I would retire to my bedroom and listen for the phone. But whenever it rang, it was always someone else.

Finally, on New Year's Eve, I called her house again and got her father, who said Caitlin wasn't home. I left a message and waited.

She didn't call back. Not that night. Not the next night.

Night after night, the same scene played itself out. Sitting up in my room waiting for her call, rationalizing why she wasn't calling when she said she would, until finally, a week and a half into the new year, I ran out of plausible explanations except for the one I had been refusing to consider. How it stung, when I admitted to myself what she was telling me. I turned off the lights in my room and lay back in bed staring up at the ceiling, wrestling with the understanding that Caitlin didn't want me. The pain was raw and vicious, as if someone had thrust a knife in my stomach and was twisting it.

To be rejected is one of life's most searing pains, especially when you're young and impressionable. It brands you. It branded me. Nearly forty years later, I can still feel it, and it doesn't feel good.

# Memory of a Summer Bike Ride

Crossing over the railroad tracks by the Gwynedd train station, I come to a narrow, wooded path that leads down to the creek below.

Another memory comes back to me, this one more pleasant. It was a hot summer afternoon during senior year in high school when Caitlin and one of her girlfriends went on a bike ride with me and my best buddy Rich. I don't know who set this up. Surely it wasn't me, shy as I was. Likely it was Rich, whom I suspect was as interested in Caitlin as I was.

However it got arranged, we met at Caitlin's house in the valley. She and her friend led the way on their bikes through secret back trails that smelled of honeysuckle and wild rose. It was brutally hot, and both girls were in shorts and halter tops, their hair flowing behind them. My buddy and I rode close behind, intoxicated. We didn't know where they were going and didn't care—we would have followed them over a cliff, if they had taken us there.

Where those girls took us, eventually, was to the place where I am now standing. It has been forty years since I walked this path, but I remember that afternoon as if it were yesterday. How hot the day was. How sweaty we were from the ride. Getting off our bikes and walking them down the path to the creek, we stripped off our sneakers and left them along with the bikes on the bank. A handmade dam of stones provided a path across a low point on the water. Caitlin went first, hopping barefoot across the stones like a sprite. Her girlfriend followed, then Rich and me. The ground on the opposite bank was soft and silty. We walked along the water's edge to a secluded deep pool beneath a high railroad pass.

I didn't know what the girls were planning, or if they were planning anything at all other than to cool off in the water. I was aware only of a fierce thrumming in my ears as I watched Caitlin tie up her T-shirt above her waist and wade out into the creek in her shorts. Her friend followed suit, while Rich and I stood back on the edge watching. A cloud of midges swirled in a slice of sunlight slanting through the trees. Dragonflies hovered above the water. The vibrato cries of cicadas rose from the surrounding trees. I had felt the strong pull of nature since I was a boy, but what I was feeling now was even more elemental and powerful.

The others in our little group must have felt it, too, the electric tension in the air. I knew Caitlin did when she turned with a smile to my buddy and said in a seductive voice, "Why don't you come over here, Rich?"

He startled as if stung by a bee and stepped toward her, but just as quickly she gave a laugh and moved away. She and her girlfriend wandered off to play in the water as if we weren't there.

The moment was broken. We were just high school friends again, out for a summer outing. Half an hour later, we came out of the water, got back on our bikes, and went our separate ways.

## The Undiscovered Country

I stand for a few minutes at the head of the wooded path reminiscing on that memory, still so fresh after all these years. Why did Caitlin turn to my friend instead of me? Had she felt any attraction to me at all, or was I simply too naïve then to have had a prayer with her? Could something different have happened that hot summer afternoon with those two girls if we two boys had been more self-confident and sexually aware?

There was sex going on in that little Catholic high school we went to, after all, but it was happening with the bad boys, the precocious boys—not with the goody two-shoes like me and Rich. Sex back then was, for us, the great undiscovered country. I was still a few years away from stepping into that country, but it would not be with Caitlin, as ardently as I fantasized that she was the one for me.

I envy people who find their partners in high school or college. To have that shared history as a ballast to your relationship must be deeply powerful and comforting as you grow older. I envy these people as well for all the pain and heartache they miss out on by choosing their partners early on and sticking with them. The quest for love is a perilous one that grounds many a ship on its shoals. Few things in life test us more than issues with relationships, particularly romantic ones.

I can attest to that. My first true romantic relationship, with a girl I met in college, triggered within me a full-blown clinical depression when the relationship came to an end. Six years later I met my future wife, a woman I thought I would be with for the rest of my life. But when that relationship, too, ended after fourteen years of marriage, I fell into an even deeper battle with the black beast that went on for four agonizing years before I was finally able to climb out of the pit.

Of course, I knew about none of these perils as a horny eighteen-year-old. I knew very little about myself at all then, really. My entire inner map of core beliefs and emotional triggers was as much undiscovered country as my sexuality. Little did I know back then that I would end up divorced and still be single here in my fifties. Little did I know that my pursuit of love over the next forty years would lead me to the heights of the mountaintop as well as to the bogs of despair. I couldn't have known that I would get so wrapped around the axle of my failing marriage that I would end up strapped to the operating table having an electric current passed through my brain in an effort to slap it out of its depressive fog.

Oh, the places we will go when we are not aware of our internal landscape. The ditches we dig for ourselves, the quarries we can allow ourselves to fall into. As I gaze down the wooded path of my past, I find myself wishing I could go back and talk to the young man I was back then. Warn him of the perils to come. Give him some sage advice on women and careers and life in general. Suggest (strongly) that he go to yoga classes and learn to meditate and take things less seriously. What pain I could have avoided for myself along the way.

But there are no playbacks in life, and it is that very pain that has led me to the lessons I can now give that younger version of myself, and to other people, too, including my own sons. The journey was necessary, I suppose. At any rate, it was the journey I was fated to walk, and all I can do now is own it and learn from it.

# 5

# Doubts and Resolutions

*Whether you believe you can do a thing or not, you are right.*

—Henry Ford

Needing to move on, I turn away from the wooded path and continue making my way up the road through the magical valley of my youth.

A monarch butterfly kicks up and swirls in front of my face, checking me out, I suppose, before unconcernedly moving off. I watch it as it flutters through the air, now alighting on a bush, now rising again, like a scrap of colored paper being blown about in the wind.

It's interesting to observe the flight of a butterfly as compared to other winged creatures such as birds and bees. A bird flies from tree to tree to achieve a purpose, much like I do when I'm commuting. Same is true for a bee traveling from hive to flower and back again.

A butterfly, on the other hand, seems to fly just for the sheer joy of flying. Yes, there is work to be done, if you consider guzzling nectar from flowers work, but let's have fun along the way. Twirl in the air, do a somersault, take a haphazard route to your destination. The hell with efficiency.

*Now that's the way to be*, I think. We Americans are altogether too consumed with getting things done. What simple blessings and beauties of life we miss along the way in our rush to achievement. The butterfly seems to have figured this out. Yeah, I want to get to that yummy flower over there, but it's such a lovely day, let's twirl through the air a bit before we go. No wonder butterflies don't have problems with stress and high blood pressure. When the rest of God's creatures have vanished from existence from working ourselves to death, the butterfly will be left to roam the Earth in a perpetual joy-fest of dancing and color.

Meanwhile, here I am, glum as Eeyore from the news I received an hour ago. How hard it is to be truly happy in this world where there are always things hitting us on the side of the head! Job issues. Financial issues. Relationship issues. Sicknesses and illnesses. Accidents. People you love getting sick and dying. Happiness is like that butterfly. It alights, dances around your head for a while, and then disappears, and you just pray and hope it will come back.

That's life, right? We come into this world trailing clouds of glory. For a brief window of time, everything is simple and carefree and magical. Then the way thickens. We move into adulthood and take on cares and responsibilities. Along the way, something is gained, but something is lost, too. We gain careers and livelihoods, homes and families, bank accounts and 401(k)s. And yet, we lose some of our childlike ability to connect to the simple joys and wonders that are unfolding in front of our eyes. Our happiness becomes conditional on situations and circumstances. As we set goals, make money, climb the corporate ladder, travel to ever-distant places, we lose connection to the present moment where we don't have to do anything, chase anything, or meet any standards or expectations to find joy. We just need to reach out and pick it.

We lose, too, some of our childlike optimism—the ability to dream big dreams unfettered by the doubts and practical considerations that come with being an adult. How simple everything seemed back then, when I was riding my bike with the wind in my face and two pretty girls in front of me! What did I know of challenges and obstacles and all the tough stuff I would face? Anything was possible. The future was an open book and there was no reason to think I couldn't write it as I wanted it to be written.

A scrap of a William Wordsworth poem that I memorized back in college English class floats back to me:

*There was a time when meadow, grove, and stream,*
*The earth, and every common sight,*

> To me did seem appareled in celestial light,
> The glory and freshness of a dream.
> It is not now as it hath been of yore.
> Turn wheresoe'er I may, by night or day,
> The things which I have seen I now can see no more.

Can we recapture that magic of our youth? I wonder as I walk. Or is it truly gone forever?

Can I still achieve my dreams? Or is it too late to even bother?

No! A stubborn voice inside me comes back. It's *never too late. Never too late to change your thinking. Never too late to start again and reinvent yourself.*

Believe it. Believe and it will be so. This new journey you're on now will lead to good places, if only you approach it with the right attitude.

## Lost in a Cloud of Doubts

So I tell myself, though even as I do so, I'm aware of the nagging doubts that eat away at my steely resolve. You're too old, you've been with one company for too long, no one will want you, you don't have the right connections, the right resumé, blah blah blah.

The doubts circle about my head like a cloud of nipping gnats. For a while, I'm lost in the dark cloud as I pass by the Gwynedd post office and continue down into the valley, until finally I realize what I'm doing and bring myself back to reality.

Jeez, cut it out, Jim! After all you've been through, after all the mountains you've climbed and swamps you've slogged through in the fifty-plus years of your life—after all the times you've doubted yourself and then proved those doubts to be unfounded again and again and again—why do you persist in not believing in yourself?

Is there any surer poison to a person's happiness and fulfillment in life than self-doubt? Caution, prudence, good judgment: All of these have obvious value in increasing our odds for surviving an often-dangerous world. But self-doubt? I'm convinced it's useless. It's worse than useless, in fact, because all it does is defeat our efforts before we even begin. Why bother attempting something if deep down inside you don't believe you'll be able to accomplish it?

If there's one thing I've learned in my time working for a big company, it's about the power of confidence. The people who accomplish things in this world are those who combine audacious dreams with the unabashed self-confidence to follow them through. Your dream, your big idea, might be the most incredible thing the world has ever seen. Your idea for a new business might one day be bigger than Facebook or Amazon. The book you're writing might be a better read and a bigger success than something from John Grisham.

But none of that matters if you lack belief in your own ability to bring your idea to fruition. There are millions of people in this world with a lot of ideas, and nowhere is it written that the good ideas will find their way to the basket while bad ones will die on the vine. In fact, some pretty mediocre ideas are able to find big markets for the simple reason that the people behind them are supremely confident and won't take no for an answer.

As for me, I have no lack of big dreams. Where I get stuck—and I suspect this is true for a lot of people—is in the confidence part. I take a shot at something, get criticized or rejected, and begin to doubt myself. Once you do that, it doesn't matter how talented you are or how good your idea is. The game is over.

## A Steely Resolve

I wasn't always like this, I reflect. Back in high school and college, I had plenty of confidence in myself and my dreams. I remember how I used to sit up in my bedroom on the second floor of the old farmhouse where I grew up writing, writing, writing. I filled up notebook after notebook with poems and short stories and drafts of novels. There was no question in my teenaged mind that I would one day become an author. I knew it as surely as I knew the sun would rise in the morning. Writing was my vocation, my calling. I would send off my poems and stories to magazines and publishers, and get back only rejection slips when the mail came in the afternoon. But I didn't let that dissuade me. In the evening, I would be writing again. Writing, revising, submitting, getting rejection slips.

Yes, I was naïve. I knew nothing of the publishing world and how hard it is to get your work noticed and in print. But still, I tried, and there's something to be said about that. Even in the first fifteen years or so while I was working for the company, I used to carve out at least an hour every morning to write before starting work. But of late, I have allowed myself to slip out of the habit. I haven't submitted a piece of my writing for publication in a couple of years.

Why? What happened?

I could blame it on the job—and it's true that finding time to write every morning has become harder as I've climbed the corporate ladder and my responsibilities have grown. But it's more than the job. The big reason I've stopped submitting my stuff is because I've lost faith in myself and my gifts. All the rejection slips wore me down. I could count on my hands and toes the number of stories and poems I've gotten published over the years, despite submitting literally hundreds of pieces to journals, agents, and publishers. When you've had that little success for over thirty-plus years of effort, you begin to question whether you have what it takes. You let those rejections get into your head. You begin to think the world is right and you are wrong and you just don't have the talent other people do.

Of course, that kind of thinking is nothing but a self-fulfilling prophecy. How can you do anything but fail in achieving your dreams if you don't believe you can do it? I think of *Chicken Soup for the Soul*, which was rejected by more than a hundred publishers before Jack Canfield finally found a house that believed in it and put it into print. The book and its countless follow-ons went on to sell hundreds of millions of copies. Now there's a *Chicken Soup* book out there for every variation of soul on the planet: kids, teenagers, couples, divorced people, teachers, gardeners, cat lovers, dog lovers, coffee lovers.

*Chicken Soup for the Soul* has become a brand of its own. It's a book-turned-leviathan. You can buy *Chicken Soup*-branded gift baskets and teddy bears. The brand even has its own line of dog and cat food. In the world of marketing, this is known as adjacency marketing. Establish a beachhead for your product and then expand into related markets that build off that core.

I'm not sure if Kitty actually feels better by eating wet food out of a *Chicken Soup for the Soul*–branded can, but still, you have to hand it to Canfield. The guy didn't give up. He refused to believe that the publishers were right and he was wrong. He believed in his talent and his vision, and that vision became real.

What I need right now, I resolve, even more than the help of a good headhunter, is a steely, unshakable confidence in my own ability to achieve whatever I set my mind on doing at this point in my life. There can be no more room for self-doubt. I need to cut any doubt out of the smithy of my soul and walk into this new phase of my journey with absolute certainty that not only will I be okay, but that I will be successful beyond my wildest dreams.

And there you have it. My first resolution on day one of my life as a free-agent remora fish.

# 6

# River of the Spirit

*All things merge into one, and a river runs through it.*

—Norman Maclean

Up ahead, I hear the trickle of running water. I am approaching a little country bridge that crosses the same creek upstream of where I walked barefoot that summer day so many years ago.

The view from the bridge is lovely, and I stop to take in the view. The creek here flows through a low-lying meadow lined with maples, birches, and soft willow trees. The trees are resplendent in their autumn dress: brilliant shades of crimson, gold, and burnished orange, lit into a fire by the afternoon sunlight.

It's like a scene out of a calendar, and I stand for a few minutes transfixed. The brilliant colors. The soft trickle of the creek. The warmth of the sun in my face. What a gorgeous day it is! I love the month of October best of all the months of the year, and this day is a true gem. My dark thoughts fly away like scattered bats before the beauty of the scene and I am transported to a place of peace, free of regrets from the past and worries about the future.

## A Moment off the Treadmill

Many times in the past, I have had glimpses of such scenes from my car window as I sped by on my drive home. But who has time to take in those scenes when you're rushing through every minute of your day? Besides, what would be accomplished by stopping on the side of the road to behold nature in its glory? What tasks would be checked off the to-do list? What progress would be made on must-do projects? What could you tangibly show for the ten minutes you wasted standing by your car door staring out at a meadow like a lost soul just released from the mental-health clinic?

Nothing. In the way such things are measured in our task-driven society, such time would be a waste. The contemplation of beauty for beauty's sake, whether in nature or art or just a good book, has taken a back seat to the ruthless pursuit of getting things done. A hundred years after the first cars rolled off Henry Ford's production line, efficiency has won the battle for the heart and soul of America. Thank you, Frederick Winslow Taylor.

Meanwhile, no one asks about the toll this takes on the humans who are part of the industrial production line. The numbers must be delivered; the shareholders must be satisfied. How exhausting it is to be a human being on this corporate treadmill! I'm exhausted, for sure. Twenty-eight years riding the back of the leviathan have worn me out.

The past year under the new management team has been particularly hard. Having to answer calls and emails on your Sunday morning when all you want to do is to have a quiet breakfast with your family. Dreading even looking at your email for fear of seeing another assignment added to your already-overloaded plate. No wonder my neck is killing me.

A lot of the people who run our modern-day corporate leviathans, I have found, just don't get that the remora fish who do their bidding are real, actual, flesh-and-blood people who have lives to live. The former CEO I worked with was one of the rare ones who *did* get it. He was demanding and set high standards for himself and others, but he also took the time to walk around the headquarters office and personally get to know the people who worked there. He prioritized that element of his job because he saw it as important to meeting his own goals. When I got the news about my cancer and had to go through colon resection surgery and six months of chemo, he took the time to check in on me and ask how I was holding up and if I needed anything.

Imagine that: a CEO asking if I needed anything from *him*!

But if you think about it, in addition to being the right thing to do, this was just smart business. When I was back from my illness, I was more committed to him and the cause than ever before. This is the way smart leaders build loyalty and productivity.

## Along the Path of a Creek

The road follows the path of the creek for a few hundred yards, and as I walk, I am treated to the lovely sound of water babbling next to me like an agreeable companion.

Is there any sound in the world more soothing than the trickle of a creek? The soft susurrus of the flowing water is tonic for the nerves as well as the soul. This is why I love fishing so much. I love to be out there on a stream in my waders with a fly rod in my hand and the water flowing around me. Catching a fish is just the icing on the cake. The cake itself, the really satisfying part, is being out in that stream, part of nature.

From the time I was young, nature has been both my balm and my inspiration. Lying in bed on the second floor of the old farmhouse, I would thrill to the wash of the wind through the trees at night, the chirping of sparrows in the cedar tree outside the window, the fury of thunderstorms in summer, the deep stillness that follows a winter snowstorm. I loved all of it. Every change of season was a new jar of delight to be opened and dug into.

Most of all I loved exploring the woods and fields that surrounded our home. I grew up on a six-acre farmette in southeastern Pennsylvania. We had a stall barn and a couple of horses and numerous nameless cats that roamed free and every spring bore litters of mewing kittens among the haybales. When I wasn't in school or doing homework, I was out walking the woods behind the horse pasture with our dog Sugar. I would be out there for countless hours, until darkness or the dinner bell would bring me home. (Yes, we actually had an old cow bell that my father affixed to a tree in the backyard to assist my mother in rounding up her brood at dinnertime. A pull of the twisted-braid rope would peal that bell for half a mile in every direction, so that pretty much everyone in our neighborhood knew when the Kerr family was having dinner.)

As it was when I was young, so it is now that I am older—the child is father of the man. I enjoy social gatherings as much as anyone, but I can't do it for long before I yearn for solitude. My sensitive nervous system craves the quiet of natural settings to bring it back to equilibrium. I make it a point every day to go into nature, usually by myself. On days when I'm too busy to get my nature time in, I can feel it, just as I feel it when I don't exercise and meditate in the morning. I'm not as calm or centered.

Some of my family and friends think I am alone too much. But there's a big difference between solitude and loneliness. Loneliness arises from a perception of being isolated and disconnected. Solitude, on the other hand, springs from a feeling of connectedness and union with something larger than ourselves. We feel most intensely lonely, I have found, when we are surrounded by people, because it is then that we most feel the contrast between our inner states and our outward circumstances.

In truth, when I am in nature, I rarely feel alone. In nature, I feel connected to a joyful, life-affirming spirit that courses through me as steadily as this little creek I'm presently walking beside. How can I be lonely when I'm connected to a life-giving spirit that flows through all things? What is there to be afraid of when I have the power of the universe flowing through me? Job loss. Illness. Divorce. Financial difficulties. Pain and suffering. All of these are nothing compared to the resources at our disposal when we are connected to the spirit.

## Link to the Spirit

I was blessed to have discovered this link to the spirit early on in my life. Once, as a boy, while out picking raspberries in the woods, I heard a wind working up in the distance. The wind pushed through the trees, growing in sound and power as it drew nearer. Then it was there, passing over me, roaring like the sea. Overhead, the canopy of trees bent before the force of the wind, setting the leaves clapping like an audience of a million hands. It seemed to me that the woods were alive, that they were infused by a consciousness that I was part of. I felt a raw, wild elation swell within me, lifting me into a higher plane of existence.

And then the wind died down, the emotion passed, and I was back on the ground, holding a container of raspberries. But something had changed within me. It was as if a veil had been lifted from my eyes and I was aware of the dual nature of reality. There was the visible world that I saw every day with my eyes, and there was the unseen inner world of feeling and emotion, and the two worlds were connected by a wellspring of spirit and joy. I knew this to be the truth, because I had felt it out there in the woods.

I carried this knowledge within me like a box of jewels as I moved toward adulthood. It was a secret that only I and the woods knew. In the greater world of people and society, I felt out of place. It was too big, too loud. I didn't seem to fit into that world very well, with my sensitivity and overreactive nervous system. Guys weren't supposed to be like this. Guys were supposed to be cool cucumbers. Risk-takers. Conquerors. Strong and steady types. That wasn't me, and it was something I had no control over.

And so, seeking belonging, I went to the woods. Nature accepted me as I was. We were alike. We were loners. We understood each other.

This spirit found in nature has held me in good stead throughout my life. I am often puzzled by the actions and motivations of people, and my own as well. But nature has never confused me. She has always been my quiet place, my therapist, my sounding board. Whenever I'm feeling down and anxious or out of sorts for a reason I cannot put my finger on, I go into nature to be free of all the noise in my head. Thinking, I have found, will only get you so far in pinpointing what is bothering you. Talking to other people, as valuable as that is, will only do so much to help you sort out your feelings and problems. The rational mind itself creates the labyrinth that it is forever working to find its way out of. To truly get to the bottom of our innermost longings and turmoil, we need to put the analytical mind aside and consult with the spirit. And for me, that can only happen in times of deep quiet.

Of course, finding this place of quiet has become infinitely harder in our media-saturated world of Facebook, Instagram, and 24/7 news channels. Maybe this is one of the reasons there is so much loneliness and desperation in the world today. We have the technological means to be constantly connected to billions of people around the world, but we have a hard time being alone with ourselves. We have lost the connection to the spirit.

## A River Runs Through Us

The sound of the trickling water draws me like the voice of a lover. I step away from the road for a brief diversion to dip my hands into the creek.

The creek water is chilly on this mid-October day, but not nearly as cold as the trout streams that I like to fish. The sunlight shimmers on the flowing surface like a liquid field of diamonds. I think of a line from *A River Runs Through It*, that wonderful book by Norman Maclean about fly fishing in Montana that became a movie with Brad Pitt: "Eventually, all things merge into one, and a river runs through it."

I really need to get back into fly fishing. I've had precious little time for it in recent years with work as crazy as it's been. To be separated from the things you enjoy is like being in prison. You feel disconnected from the source of your life, your joy. The days become gray and sunless. Even as you run ever faster on the hamster wheel to meet the day's responsibilities and obligations, time slows down. You want the day to be over, the week to be over, so you can get to a place of centeredness and equilibrium.

When I'm out on a stream with a fly rod, on the other hand, life flows. I'm not even aware of the time because I'm immersed in the present moment. That's what it's like to be in the spirit. Time dissolves. All things merge into one: the external world and the internal world, the past and the future, the world that was and the world that will be. It's all right there in the river.

There's much to be learned by spending time on rivers. The biggest lesson is about the passing nature of things. A river is always changing. The stream that I have my hands in today is not the same stream that I was walking in that hot summer day thirty-some years ago while out riding with my high school friends. It may appear to be same stream. It may flow through the same territory and have the same banks and structure and name. But the water itself—that which makes a stream a stream—is entirely different every time we step into it.

It is that constant change and flow that keeps a river healthy. The insect life, the minnows that feed on the insects, the trout that feed on the minnows and insects: The entire river ecosystem depends on the continual flow of the water. As long as the current is flowing, things stay healthy. Stop the flow and the river dies. The water gets backed up and turns stale. You won't catch any trout in those waters.

The same holds true for us humans. A river runs through us. Our blood flows through our arteries like a stream. Our thoughts and emotions flow like a stream. It only makes sense; after all, we came from the oceans millions of years ago. As long as the blood keeps moving and the thoughts and emotions keep moving, we stay healthy and happy. It's when things get stopped up that we get into trouble. The springs cease flowing, the current stops, and the river of the spirit turns into a putrid, festering swamp. Vibrant health becomes sickness and disease.

## The Swamp of Human Desperation

How well I know that swamp of human desperation, having spent years of my life wallowing there. There is no running water in that place, no light or life, no joy or pleasure. The swamp is the opposite of all of those things. It's a dark, barren place: stagnant, fetid, putrid. Not even maggots can survive there. All is dead except for the black beast, and the black beast wanted me dead, too.

When I experienced my first clinical depression in my early twenties, the discovery that this godforsaken place existed, in a world that I naïvely thought was blessed and benevolent, shook my worldview to the core. Now, in retrospect, it makes sense to me. Nothing can exist without its opposite. Light cannot exist without shadow. Good cannot exist without the presence of evil, or how would we even know what good is? We cannot have pleasure without pain, joy without suffering. In everything is bound both thesis and its antithesis; it's just a matter of the degree to which they are present in each moment.

But I didn't understand that then. All I knew was that everything was dark and everything hurt. Even my thoughts hurt. How could that be? How could a thought hurt?

Thoughts were supposed to come and go, but now they were being shot through my guts like piercing arrows. I wanted only to get away from this onslaught, to find a place of safety where the arrows couldn't reach me. But there was no escape. How do you get away from your own thoughts? I was a duck in my own barrel.

I remember, in the thick of my suffering, raging against the God I had always believed in. *What have I done to deserve this hell I'm living in? Why would an all-good, all-loving God be doing this to me? I'm a good person!*

It was only when I had journeyed through the land of the black beast a second time, in my forties, that I began to understand that God had nothing to do with why I was there. The suffering I was going through had nothing to do with whether or not I was a good person. It was my thinking. My unconscious beliefs, my distorted perceptions, my mishandled emotional reactions. I had manifested all of it. I had manifested the dark, painful periods of my life just as I had manifested the bright, joyful ones.

I was the manifester of most everything I had experienced in my life. I just didn't realize I was doing it.

## Meditations on the Nature of Spirit

Another line from Maclean's *A River Runs Through It* comes to me: "We can love completely what we cannot completely understand."

It's true. We don't need to understand something to love it. But when we do not understand where our joy is coming from, it's easy to get disconnected from what we love and allow other things to slip into its place. Things like money, status, titles, big houses, expensive cars, trophy wives. The problem with all those things is they can always be taken away, and most surely will be during our mortal lives. So hinging our happiness on them is like building our house in the ocean on pillars made of sand.

Material things are all poor substitutes for the real thing, which is the spirit that brings us joy. Lose that connection to the spirit and our days lose their luster. We slog through our days, rather than enjoying them.

That's the place where I was at in those dark years I spent in the swamp, wrestling with the black beast. I was disconnected from the source of my joy. I dwelt in a world of un-spirit, of un-joy.

And if the swamp of human desperation is the antithesis of spirit, I ask myself, then what is the thesis? What is spirit? What exactly is this thing that I felt first as a boy and that has carried me through so much tough stuff in my life?

I gaze down at the glistening water, mulling on this question, and I realize I don't have a good answer for it. It seems to be one of those profoundly unanswerable questions, like asking someone the meaning of life. What is spirit? Where does it come from? What is the source behind the spring?

Is spirit an emotion or a feeling? A deeply felt sense of joy like what I experienced out there in the woods as a boy picking raspberries?

Yes, it is that, but it is also more than that. To call spirit a feeling is too limiting. Joy and elation are what you feel when you're in the spirit, but they are not the spirit itself.

Is spirit a place? Spirit seems connected somehow with nature and the wilderness, since it is so often in nature that

I have felt the stirrings of spirit. But I have felt it in other places and situations as well, such as while writing or listening to music.

Is spirit the province of religion? I think of the times I felt the spirit rise while sitting in church hearing the swell of choir music, or standing in a European cathedral staring awestruck at the majestic stained glass overhead. But this isn't all of spirit, either, because I know from experience that religion can just as easily stifle the expression of spirit with its rigid rules and dogma.

Is spirit a divine being—God, Jesus Christ, Allah, Muhammed, the Buddha?

It's a bit of a puzzle. I know spirit by its qualities but not by its substance. Spirit is joyful, positive, hopeful, life-giving. It is abundant and lacks nothing. It's profound, but also light as snow. It's deep, but also playful. It's simple, but also contains multitudes.

Spirit is also free—this I know for a fact. Spirit seeks flow, like this stream I'm standing next to. Try to force it, or constrain it, or control it in any way, and spirit slips through your hands. Spirit is like that butterfly I saw on the road a couple of miles back, dancing joyfully on the breeze, in touch with something that I, deep in my worry, am not.

That's it, I think. That's what spirit is. Spirit is not a person, place, or thing. It's a state of deep connection to a universal life-giving source that runs through all living things. I think of the times in my life when I have been in spirit, how I felt lifted into a higher plane of existence. The "I" that was myself melted away and was subsumed into something infinitely larger and more powerful. I became that something larger, and it became me. There was a merging that happened then, such as what Maclean wrote about in his book. It was a state of great power. Nothing could stop me when I was in the spirit, because there was nothing outside of me that could stop me.

It makes no sense, really, any of it, not to the rational mind. But for anyone who has felt it, who has been in that place of the spirit, it all makes perfect sense. Spirit is a state of deep connectedness and union with a divine source of abundance, hope, strength and power: free-flowing and freely given.

And the wonderful news, the happy news, is that spirit is always available to us. Even in the darkest, most arid periods of our lives when everything feels pointless, the spirit is quietly babbling deep within us, bidding us to go on. When my exhausted mind told me there was no hope left but to drive my car into the local quarry, the spirit wouldn't let me give up. When I was sitting in the chemo chair having poisons pumped into my veins, the spirit told me I would be all right, that I had a lot of life yet to live.

As I watch the gurgling stream flow through the pleasant meadow, I give silent thanks that I was able to find my way out of the black swamp and back to life. It took a lot of work to get there, but it was worth it, just to be standing here at this moment enjoying this fine day.

I need to do some of that inner work again now, I think. I'm not clinically depressed, thank God, but I've definitely lost my spark. All work and no play has burned me to a cinder.

I need to reconnect with my spirit again. No company or job can do that for me. It's up to me.

# 7

# Brands and Bean Burritos

*Getting and spending, we lay waste our powers;*
*Little we see in Nature that is ours;*
*We have given our hearts away, a sordid boon!*

—William Wordsworth

Spurred on by my little internal pep talk, I leave the creek and begin working my way up a long, grueling hill out of the mystical valley of Gwynedd.

The hill never felt all that steep to me during the years that I was driving it. Walking it, however, is a different matter, and I'm grateful that I've kept myself in decent shape over the years. I am a bit of a fanatic when it comes to exercising. Four or five days a week, I get up at the ungodly hour of four-thirty in the morning to get to the gym when it opens at five. Call me crazy (many people do, including my kids), but I've been at this routine for so long that I can hardly think of another way to start my workday.

I exercise not just for the physical benefits, but for the stamina it gives me to handle the stresses of life as a corporate remora fish. It takes a lot of mental endurance to work in the corporate world, especially when you're working for a company that is forever restructuring and downsizing. As hard as it is to drag myself out of a warm bed at four-thirty on cold winter mornings, I am always glad afterward that I've made the effort. On days when I don't do it, I don't feel as clear-headed, confident, and productive. And isn't that what the leviathan wants from us—productivity?

## Out of the Valley

At the crest of the hill, I emerge onto the highway, thus completing my nearly four-mile scenic loop through the valley. But there is no avoiding congestion now. I am on U.S. Route 202, which around these parts is pretty much synonymous with congestion.

Route 202 holds the distinction of running through some of the most heavily populated territory in the Northeast. It starts down in Delaware and meanders north through eight states all the way up to Maine, connecting all kinds of vital cities and towns along the way. As a result, Route 202 it is a popular artery for suburbanites like me commuting to and from their places of work in the tristate region of Pennsylvania, Delaware, and New Jersey.

The problem is, the road was never designed to handle all this commuter traffic in addition to the poor locals just trying to get from their house to the grocery store. There are more lights on Route 202 than on a Christmas tree, and at rush hour, these lights turn into bottlenecks that are enough to try a yogi's patience.

The place I'm now walking is one such well-known chokepoint. It's where a four-lane stretch of highway bumps down into two lanes for a mile or so before widening out again. Many an evening commute have I spent here in my car in long lines of traffic waiting for the signal to cycle through round after round of light changes, before finally I get my chance to break free.

Perhaps the one consolation of sitting at this intersection is the view it gives of the gorgeous William Penn Inn, a three-hundred-year-old tavern that goes back to the days of the original Quaker pilgrims who settled Penn's Woods. With its white stucco walls accented by black shutters, the huge inn is as much a feast for the eyes as it is for the stomach. At night, the building as well as the stately sycamore tree in front are lit with tens of thousands of white bulbs, which makes for quite the scene from the road.

The inn is especially lovely over the holidays. There's something cozy about getting dressed up on a crisp December night and going to the William Penn Inn to sit at the old oak bar with a glass of wine in your hand, listening to the piano man in a tux playing holiday tunes while lights twinkle outside the window. While on the pricey side, the fare there is excellent and, in my book, well worth the money. The environment alone is worth the price of admission. I'm generally a frugal person—it's the Scot in me—but I also appreciate the finer things in life. What good is working so hard for your money if you don't enjoy it?

## Malls, Macy's, and Everywhere a Sign

Leaving the upscale inn, I continue north along the busy highway.

With every step I take, the area gets more built up. Bucolic scenes of rolling hayfields and meandering creeks give way to storefronts and strip malls. I pass Bacco's Italian restaurant, a Wawa convenience store, a Rite Aid pharmacy. Traffic lights and busy intersections slow my progress. I am entering Montgomeryville, a sprawling complex of shopping plazas, restaurants, and you-name-it other establishments catering to every need, whim, and budget. Over the years, I have seen Montgomeryville expand from a lazy strip of roadside establishments to a retail shopping mecca second only in this county to the great King of Prussia mall.

This is good news for shoppers, but a nightmare for commuters. Five major roads come together here in Montgomeryville—Route 202 among them. Until a recent bypass road was completed to relieve some of the traffic flow, I drove through Montgomeryville most days on my commute home. The exception was during the holidays, when I did everything within my power to avoid this area. Driving through Montgomeryville during the mad holiday shopping rush is enough to suck the spirit out of Santa Claus. Traffic around here pretty much comes to a standstill in December, when a decision to drive through Montgomeryville becomes a gamble whose odds are stacked against you.

The spark that lit the fire of this commercial expansion was the construction in the 1970s of the Montgomery Mall, which I am now passing. The two-story structure was built at a time when suburban retail malls were sprouting up across America to satisfy the country's rapidly growing appetite for shopping. I was a teenager then, and I remember all the excitement in the air when this bright new complex went up on what used to be an open farm field. This mall was more than just a place to shop. It was a place to eat and mingle and socialize. My friends and I would go there to hang out in high school. My mother and her girlfriends would meet at the mall for their daily walks. When I had a family of my own, we would pack up the stroller and go to the mall on Friday nights to walk the kids and eat at the food court.

Over the years, most of the original hundred-plus stores in the mall have swapped out as retail tastes changed. Bamberger's became Macy's. Wanamaker's became Hecht's, then Strawbridge's, then Boscov's. Sears stayed, well, Sears, and eventually closed up altogether. Stores came and went, but the experience of shopping the mall stayed the same.

Tell someone you were going to the mall and they knew what that meant. You went to the mall for the shared communion of shopping with other people. You went to find out what other people were buying and wearing and eating and talking about.

Alas, the mall is no longer that center of shared shopping experience: The advent of the Internet and Amazon has seen to that. The cavernous mall parking lot is nowhere near as full as it used to be. The building itself looks tired, despite the best efforts of new tenants such as Wegmans to breathe new life into it. Today's suburban dwellers don't want the one-stop-shopping experience of a mall; they can get that by going online. Who wants to waste an hour walking around a mall in the hopes of finding something when you can get what you need at the lowest price on Amazon and have it shipped for free to your house in a day or two?

That's me, at least. When it comes to shopping, I am a dyed-in-the-wool utilitarian. I shop as little as I have to, to buy only what I absolutely need, while aiming to extract the greatest amount of value I can from the transaction. I feel about shopping the way I feel about commuting or a visit to the dentist office: I want to get through it as quickly as possible with the least amount of pain.

## The Brand-Stamping Marketing Machine

Still, it's hard, so extraordinarily hard, to remain a stoic utilitarian shopper in a society that is intent on separating you from your money. As I walk through the suburban shopping mecca of Montgomeryville, familiar brand names catch my eye: Starbucks, Wegmans, Payless, Marriott, Verizon Wireless, Best Buy, Firestone, Rite Aid, HomeGoods. It's amazing how many signs you see when you're walking. Each one means something to me. I know what every one of these brands offers, what I can get by walking through their doors.

It strikes me, in a way it never has before, that behind each of these signs is a multibillion-dollar leviathan with thousands of remora fish riding its back. Behind each one of those companies is a marketing machine intent on stamping its brand on the minds of the consumer, which is us. Because the majority of Americans work for big companies, that means we are feeding on both ends of the whale. By day, we work for the company; by night, we buy from it.

Having worked for nearly thirty years in the field of marketing, I can appreciate the success of these companies in conveying the essence of their respective value propositions through a clever mix of colors and typefaces. Still, it bothers me at a certain level to have surrendered a piece of my psyche to a corporation. Is this not the human equivalent of a steer having its hide stamped by a hot branding iron?

I am aware of an inner voice raising protest. I am not a dumb, driven cow! I will not be owned!

But I am. We all are. To live in today's modern society is to have our mental landscape parceled up among dozens of brands that spend a ton of money to get our attention. It's a competition for eyeballs. Every time we drive (or walk, as is the case for me this day) through a shopping district like this one, our attention is being vied for. Whenever we turn on the television, computer, or smartphone, we are in some way being pitched. We are human eyeballs in a marketing ping-pong game designed to get us to buy things we don't need and often don't even want.

The sophistication of this marketing machine has increased immensely in my lifetime, to the point where it's becoming really, really hard to escape. Our homes are certainly not sanctuaries, not as long as we have any kind of device turned on. The ads come at us in clever ways intended to catch us unawares, so we don't even know we're being sold to. Traffic updates are brought to you by Brand X. The Defensive Play of the Game is brought to you by Brand Y.

Leviathans—they're all leviathans.

The other day as I was watching the six o'clock news on my favorite local TV station, the programming slipped into what I thought was a special report with a panel of experts talking about a revolutionary new anti-aging approach for skin care. I quickly realized this wasn't news at all but a cleverly disguised sponsored two-minute advertisement aimed at selling a skin cream. How much did that company spend for the segment? Likely millions. Whatever it was, I'm sure it paid for itself in multiples.

When I was growing up, there were only a handful of television channels to choose from. The TV was in the corner of the living room and it stayed there when we left the room. Today, the media channels are everywhere: in our homes, our cars, our places of work. They're in the stores where we shop, the restaurants where we eat, the gas pumps where we fill up our vehicles. We carry the media with us wherever we go with our smartphones, our smart watches.

## Advertising Jingles and Algorithms

There's no denying the power of a clever advertising message in stamping a brand on an impressionable mind. To this day, I still sometimes find myself unconsciously humming jingles that I heard decades ago:

> "Oh, I wish I were an Oscar Mayer wiener."
> "The best part of waking up is Folgers in your cup."
> "In the valley of the—ho-ho-ho!—Green Giant!"
> "I am stuck on Band-Aid brand 'cause Band-Aid's stuck on me."

Who can say how many Green Giant or Band-Aid products I've bought over the years because of those catchy jingles? Who can say how many times I've snubbed alternative brands of hot dogs, coffee, frozen vegetables, and bandages because of the power that those jingles held over my unconscious perceptions and preferences?

And if those early mass-market campaigns worked as well as they did on me forty years ago, imagine how much more powerful today's campaigns must be in stamping brands on impressionable minds. The marketing campaigns of the 1960s and 1970s were conceived in the offices of powerful New York City advertising agencies by men and women (mostly men) sitting around smoky conference rooms brainstorming ways to create a jingle that resonated with the masses—à la *Mad Men*.

Today's campaigns make use of highly sophisticated algorithms, bots, and web cookies that track our every click, search, view, and purchase. This history gets fed into automated marketing databases filled with reams of information about me, about you, about all of us. Data about our income. Our location. Our demographics. Our buying patterns and preferences.

All of this rich information allows today's big companies to be much more precise and targeted in their marketing efforts, to the point of being able to offer up personalized campaigns and advertisements aimed at "markets of one." Modern leviathans rely on these databases and marketing engines to satisfy their voracious appetites for growth. Data represent the new capital of the twenty-first century, arguably even more important than traditional forms of capital. Data capital provides the rich, life-sustaining protein that gives today's leviathans their fat. Where schools of data krill swim through the waters of the marketplace, there you will find the big companies voraciously feeding.

Oh, I know all about this because I work every day in this world of corporate marketing. Because I work in this world, I have become much more attuned to how clever, and often insidious, these campaigns truly are. The messages come at us from the time we wake up to the moment we lay our heads down on the pillow at night. Clickbait is everywhere, trying to draw us in. Stories on the Kardashians and the Jenners.

Videos of cute little babies and kittens and puppies waking up their owners in the morning. To watch the video, you first have to watch the advertisement, which launches on autoplay at very high volume, but when you go to silence the damn thing, the mute button mysteriously vanishes for a few critical seconds from the control panel, so you're stuck watching the ad until the video comes on, which is exactly what the advertiser wants you to do so as to brand its name and message indelibly on the landscape of your consciousness.

## More Convenience, Less Peace of Mind

Make no mistake: The entire purpose of this marketing machine is to influence our thinking and behavior. It is to make us less aware in our moment-to-moment buying decisions. It's to play with our subconscious so that the next time we are thinking about buying something, the brand's name will come to the top of our mental list of options in that particular category of goods or services. And once it gets us to buy, the marketing machine's intent is to lock us in via long-term contracts, autopay, monthly subscriptions, loyalty points programs, and other means where we equally don't pay attention.

All this is done under the guise of making our lives easier and more convenient. And, in many ways, the marketing machine delivers on that promise. It's nice being able to watch movies on demand. It's nice being able to have books and gifts and groceries delivered to our door. It's nice being able to play music at the touch of a button.

But all this comes at a cost that goes well beyond the money we spend on these services. There's a cost in terms of our peace of mind. As powerful as our human brains are, we only have so much mental space to devote to things during the course of our waking day. Every time we engage with the marketing machine, every time we see the ads and pull out our credit card for another product or service that we don't really need, we are carving out another piece of our mental space for the purpose of tending to that product or service and taking care of the monthly bills that come with them. The more mental space we devote to that stuff, the less is available for other important priorities, such as talking to our spouse and children or pursuing a hobby that gives us satisfaction.

Is it any wonder that our sense of overwhelm is so great in today's world? The more ease and convenience we get with every new gadget and service sold to us by the marketing machine, the greater our sense of complexity and overwhelm grows. I know that is the case for me, at least. Being highly sensitive by nature, my nerves can only stand so much before they revolt. There are days when I want to just throw up my hands and scream, STOP! Stop sending me bills! Stop sending me email offers! Stop charging my credit card or bank account every month! I'm busy enough trying to keep up with work and emails and demanding, unreasonable executives. I just want a moment's peace where I don't have to be thinking about all this stuff!

The worst part, in my book, is being constantly, relentlessly, mercilessly sold to. Sold to in the morning. Sold to at night. Sold to on weekdays. Sold to on weekends. The robo-calling telemarketers are at the top of my evil list. Despite having placed my phone number umpteen times on "Do Not Call" lists, I regularly field calls late into the evening from robotic voices trying to get me to call some number or click some link or vote for some politician I don't know.

Not far behind the telemarketers on my evil list are the telecommunications companies. With all the telco mergers over the past twenty years, there are only a few of the big boys left, and these leviathans are absolute masters at the art of selling. First, they draw you in with some juicy offer to trade in your paid-up phone for the latest, greatest smartphone model, even though your old phone is working just fine. But when you get to the store, they inform you that your old phone isn't part of the trade-in offer and you'll need to pay seven hundred bucks to get that cool new phone. Since by now you're sold and really, really want the phone, you go for it, putting it on the monthly installment plan along with that juicy all-you-can-eat, eight-gig-per-month data plan. By the time you walk out of the store, you've signed up for a monthly bill of a hundred bucks.

And that's just for the phone service, mind you. I use Verizon for both my phone service and my home TV/Internet service, and between the two services, I'm paying this company a minor mortgage payment every month. There's no discount for being a customer of both because, well, Verizon FIOS is a different leviathan from Verizon Wireless and they work off different systems, different accounts, different pricing structures.

Meanwhile, for all that money you're paying every month, good luck trying to get through to someone if you have a problem or a question. In fact, good luck even locating a contact number on your bill to call. That information is hidden deep in the small print because the fact of the matter is, the phone company really doesn't *want* you calling. They want you to fill out the contact form on the website or go to their online "support community" for the answer. Do the work yourself, in other words. It's cheaper for them, and it's all about cost-efficiency, remember?

But no—you really want to talk to someone. What are all these fees on my bill? Why are they charging me for three set-top boxes when I only have two in my house? Why am I not getting the Showtime channel anymore, when I always used to? So you hunt down the phone number in the fine print and give it a call and suddenly you find yourself trying to communicate with a computerized woman's voice. The conversation goes something like this:

*Tell me what you are looking to do. For example, I want to learn about Verizon Premium movie channels.*
I want to speak to someone about my bill.
*Billing. You have a question about your bill?*
Yes. I want to speak to someone about my bill and why it's so high.
*Your current bill is one hundred thirty-eight dollars and forty-six cents. I see that your bill is due. Would you like to pay it now?*

> No, the bill isn't right. I'm not going to pay that.
> Payment. You want to make a payment?
> No! I want to speak to a real, live person about my services.
> Services. You want information about Verizon services?

When you finally say the magic word—Representative!—that will put you in touch with a real person, another voice comes on to tell you that the company is experiencing higher than normal call volume but please hold on because your business is important to us. While you wait, the singsong computerized woman's voice tells you about some cool new Verizon service that you can sign up for to add to the gouging you're already getting. By the time you finally get to a real person, you're ready to leap snarling across that crystal-clear 4G telephone line to throttle the poor soul on the other end who himself is overworked and doesn't deserve the tongue-lashing you're giving him, except that he represents the Evil Empire that is putting you through these nine circles of hell.

Sell, sell, sell. The entire modern marketing machine is designed to sell. Even that poor customer-service representative, who is so apologetic for the issues you've been having and is trying to bring you back from the brink of tossing your phone into the nearest river and entering a monastery, even he at some point, before this phone call is over, will try a not-so-subtle attempt to get you to buy some cool new service that will add to your already-bloated bill, because that is what he has been trained to do.

## Lost in the Labyrinth

Unless you live off the grid without Internet service, you are subject to this marketing machine. You walk with me through this labyrinth of brands that seek our attention and eyeballs. Signs, signs, everywhere a sign. They clutter our walks, our drives, our screens, our minds.

The purpose of this marketing machine is to make buyers of us by drawing us into the classic sales funnel.* In case you're not familiar with it, the sales funnel is an extremely powerful technique used by the biggest companies in the world to fuel their growth. It starts with awareness, moves through consideration and conversion, and takes us into the marketer's nirvana of loyalty, where the consumer becomes an advocate for the brand, telling their friends and family how wonderful the product is.

It's all extremely sophisticated. It needs to be that way because the whale, remember, needs lots of krill to keep growing and making its numbers, and the sales funnel is the hand that feeds the beast. The funnel creates the pipeline of future deals and customers that drive revenue, margins, and profit, so that when the CEO and chief financial officer get on the next quarterly earnings call with investors, they can report numbers that will meet Wall Street expectations and keep that stock price going up so they can hang on to their jobs and make their bonuses at the end of the year.

At the center of this marketing brand machine—highly automated, powered by algorithms and bots, funded by

---

* See the Appendix for more on the sales funnel.

multimillion-dollar budgets and overseen by some of the smartest marketers and data scientists in the world—is us.

That's you and me. We are "the Consumer," spelled with a capital C. We who consume. Not we who create, but we who consume. We who consume with our eyes and ears and our other senses, all of which are played like fiddle strings by the brands that seek a share of our attention and our wallets.

We not only work for the leviathans; we are the krill that feeds them. We serve both ends of the equation. The left hand feedeth us; the right hand taketh from our pockets.

## Simplify, Simplify!

Thoreau went to live in a cabin in the Massachusetts woods to get away from all this consumerism. I think of him sitting alone in that tiny hand-built cabin scribbling down his bare-minimum list of items needed to get through the winter, along with the cost of each one. The point he was trying to make with his "experiment" in the woods was that human beings in actuality need very little to be safe, healthy, and happy. There are, he wrote, only four true "necessaries of life": food, shelter, clothing, and fuel. Through his experiment, he aimed to show that all these necessaries can be had readily enough without having to go into debt.

Every frill we add to our lives beyond the essentials carries a cost well beyond its sticker price: the cost of the time and labor we put into making the money needed to pay for those frills. It's when we live beyond our means and have to resort to borrowing that we get ourselves in trouble.

Credit leads to debt, which leads to obligation, which leads to enslavement. When we are in debt, we are enslaved not only to the bank that issued us the credit card, but also to the company that employs us. I owe, I owe, it's off to work I go.

*Simplify, simplify!* was Thoreau's rallying cry to his fellow Americans. You are working your fingers to the bone to pay for things that you do not need, and all this stuff is weighing you down like a bunch of pack horses. You only have one life, only so much time on this planet. Don't make the Faustian bargain of handing over your most precious asset to an unfeeling corporation in exchange for a lot of stuff you don't need.

But how hard that is! How very hard. There are so many ways for the marketing machine to get to us in our modern, media-soaked age. We have little chance but to be influenced by it. We the Consumer, with our desire for acceptance and approval, our need to keep up with the Joneses, our tendency to buy into powerfully told narratives—how can we not get sucked into the marketing funnel and become krill for the leviathan? Who among us does not pull out his credit card when he is being told (a) he really needs this product and (b) he is likely never to see a deal like this one again? Who among us has the willpower and the discipline to resist the impulse to buy something that promises to make our lives, and the lives of our children, better, safer, easier, and more convenient, even if that purchase adds to the debt that weighs heavily on our minds and keeps us going back to the job that we really don't want to be doing, and probably wouldn't be doing, if we didn't have such a big credit-card payment to make at the end of the month?

We're only human, after all. We have needs and longings that go well beyond the four spare "necessaries" that Thoreau laid out in *Walden*: needs for love, for belonging, for connection, for fulfillment. The modern marketing machine is well aware of this. These needs and belongings, too, are factored into the algorithms and sophisticated automation tools used by the modern-day marketing machine, which is set up to play on those strings, for the purposes of getting us to buy, buy, buy.

Our only chance, our only defense against the machine, is conscious awareness. By being more aware of the myriad ways that modern brands are attempting to get inside our heads and influence our purchasing behaviors, the more we move from types to individuals, from consumers to creators.

The more aware we become of the tradeoffs we're making every time we choose a product that we want but really don't need, the more we reclaim our power as individuals.

Through conscious awareness, we move from consumers to creators—from suckerfish relying on the fat of leviathans, to free-swimming fish in charge of our destinies, swimming in the direction of our hopes and dreams.

## Dominoes of Unconscious Choices

*And you, Jim, I ask myself: What would Henry David say if he were walking here beside you today through this carnival of shopping delights?*

I hope he wouldn't be too tough on me. I am, all in all, a frugal person. I like nice stuff as much as the next guy, but I don't want a lot of it. I hate being sold to and don't much care about impressing people with the stuff I wear, own, or drive. I drive Fords because I find them to be the most reliable car for the money. I tend to wear the same set of clothes day after day. I would rather spend my hard-earned money on something of quality, and use it until it's worn out, than have a closet full of stuff I rarely put on.

Still, I have succumbed more times than I care to admit to the pressures of keeping up with the Joneses. I think of the things that I have bought over the years that I didn't really need but that put me into some form of enslavement: the home I'm currently living in, for instance. It's a beautiful Cape Cod, in a great neighborhood, within walking distance of the high school where my three sons went. I bought it soon after my divorce, because I wanted my kids to feel they could continue to have nice things and live in a higher-end area despite the breakup of their family home. But I overpaid for the house and surely will never get back the money I have put into it.

I realize now that my judgment at the time was clouded by a desire to impress my sons, to make them feel I was able to continue providing for them despite the misfortune of the divorce. But what did that matter, really? The four of us could have lived just as well and happily in a townhouse. What mattered was that they knew I wasn't going away and would continue to love them and be involved in their lives.

In the meantime, my decision to take on a big mortgage, along with all the expenses that go along with owning a bigger house, added to my financial responsibilities, which in turn demanded that I hold down a high-paying job, which in turn was why I needed to spend so much time commuting back and forth to work for a big company, which was why I had so little time to do other things I really wanted to do. Like write.

And so on and so forth. Such are the dominoes of unconscious choices that lead us, one by one, down into the dungeon of debt and enslavement.

I can hear Thoreau's voice exhorting me from the woods of Concord: *Simplify, simplify!*

Well, I have no choice but to simplify now, don't I? Maybe I'll sell everything and go live in a rented one-bedroom apartment. Live on oatmeal and canned vegetables and black-bean burritos bought for a buck from the value menu at Taco Bell.

Ah, the power of subliminal advertising. I realize I'm thinking about burritos because there is a Taco Bell just up ahead. I love Taco Bell black-bean burritos with chipotle sauce. I haven't eaten lunch and my stomach gives an anticipatory rumble at the thought of biting into one of those burritos.

But then I remember that I'm about to lose my job and the next college tuition payment is due in a month.

A buck is a buck. I skip the burrito and continue walking.

# 8

## Bob Marley and Matters of the Mind

*O the mind, mind has mountains; cliffs of fall*
*Frightful, sheer, no-man-fathomed. Hold them cheap*
*May who ne'er hung there.*

—Gerard Manley Hopkins

Leaving the heart of Montgomeryville without making a purchase, I make a series of well-practiced zigzag moves around a Best Buy store, a Home Depot, and an AMC movie theater—all for the purpose of avoiding the dreaded Five Points intersection.

Five Points is where Route 202 meets Routes 309 and 463, a multiplication of three-digit highways that equates to a lot of waiting. I like to refer to the Five Points intersection as Five Minutes, because it takes at least that long to get through the traffic signals that rule over the intersection like peevish little dictators. If there is one thing that drives me crazy more than anything in our modern, computer-driven world, it's having my precious time lorded over by a steel box filled with sensors and wires taking its good old time working through its sequence of red, yellow, and green lights.

I mean, I get the importance of traffic signals to keep our congested roads from descending into chaos. We need these things to function in an advanced society. But still—we are intelligent creatures, aren't we? There is something profoundly dehumanizing about being told what to do on the road by a bunch of dumb signals hanging from wires.

There's a part of me that wants to rebel against the system like Winston in the novel 1984. But I would only be crushed, as poor Winston ultimately was, so the best I can do is avoid intersections like Five Points that steal away my precious time. I estimate that over my years of commuting through Montgomeryville to and from work, my Five Points avoidance strategy has given me back perhaps a full day of life that I would have otherwise spent waiting for a steel box to give me permission to proceed.

In the course of twenty-eight years, one day may not seem like very much. But in the course of a limited lifetime, every day is golden.

# Sleepwalking on Route 202

Beyond the Home Depot and AMC movie theater, I get back onto Business Route 202 and continue my journey north. I have been walking now for three hours and am more than halfway home. The sun, which was directly overhead when I started out from the office, is beginning to slant down in the western sky.

Thank goodness I wore my cushy shoes to work today. Thank goodness, too, that it's a cool day or I'd be sweating like a horse and this would be no fun at all. As it is, I'm rather enjoying the walk, until my mind slips back into worry mode and I get to thinking again about what I'm going to do when the company lets me go, what's going to happen to me and my boys, how I'm going to take care of them and pay for their college tuitions, let alone fund my own retirement so I don't have to work until I'm ninety.

What happens if I can't find a new job? How long will my savings last? Should I put the house on the market now before the real-estate market dries up over the holidays?

Round and round the mind goes, blending its foul-tasting concoction of regrets, fears, insecurities, and self-reproach that steals our ability to be truly present in the moment. For the next half an hour or so, I am so caught up in all my worries that I barely notice where I am or what's going on around me, until finally, another couple of miles up the road, I realize what I'm doing and bring myself back to awareness.

Turning, I look back at the stretch of territory I have just unconsciously passed without really seeing. I note the golden arches of a McDonald's, and the Wells Fargo bank branch where I have stopped many a time on the way home from work to grab cash from the ATM. I have no recollection of having just passed those establishments, or the Firestone dealer across the street from them, or the housing development farther back up the road.

It's amazing what the mind will do when left unchecked. For all I know, a gang of bank robbers was pulling a heist at that Wells Fargo as I was passing and I didn't notice because I was so lost in my head. It strikes me that all that stuff I've been thinking and worrying about for the past half-hour isn't real. It doesn't exist. It's all mental vaporware. Yes, I will be losing my job of twenty-eight years, and yes, that will have financial implications for me, my kids, and our lifestyle. But it hasn't happened yet. It's in the future, and the future exists only in the mind.

Likewise, all the things I'm regretting, all the decisions I've made or didn't make and the reasons why I did or didn't make them—that stuff isn't real, either. It's in the past, and the past exists only in my head. I can do nothing about the past except learn from it, and as for the future, what good will worrying do? What purpose will it serve? What problems will it solve?

None. Nada. The past half-hour of regretting and worrying has served no purpose but to take me away from the beauty of the present moment to a negative inner space that feels crappy. How silly. And how often does this same scenario happen during the course of the average day or week or year? A lot. Multiply my half-hour of sleepwalking by thousands of such lost, unconscious moments over the course of my life and you're talking about a lot of wasted time and energy.

It's not just in getting and spending or waiting at traffic lights that we waste our powers. We waste them in worrying, and that's something, unfortunately, that I am rather good at. I think of the terrible states my mind has gotten itself into over the years with all its worrying. What things could I have accomplished if only I had doubted less and believed more? I've lost literally years of my life in worry-induced states of abject anxiety and misery, and it was all over nothing.

No more of that, I resolve. I can't lose any more of my precious days by regretting the past or worrying about the future. Things will work out. I won't starve. I will get my kids through college. Look at the birds of the air. They neither sow nor reap nor gather into barns, yet our heavenly father feeds them.

Have faith. Don't worry, be happy.

And just like that, the words of the Bob Marley song pop into my head:

*Rise up this morning*
*Smiled with the rising sun.*
*Three little birds*
*Pitch by my doorstep.*
*Singin' sweet songs*
*Of melodies pure and true.*

Ah, good old Bob Marley, who died at the tragically young age of thirty-six from cancerous rot of the toe, yet whose music never fails to lighten the heart:

*Don't worry about a thing,*
*'Cause every little thing's going to be all right . . .*

## The Roller-Coaster Ride of the Wandering Mind

And so, ridiculously humming Bob Marley on a day when I ought to be crying in my beer, I turn forward again and continue making my way homeward while reflecting on this strange and marvelous creation called the mind.

It's amazing, the roller-coaster ride that our minds put us through. One minute you're down in the dumps about something, thinking it's the most awful thing that's ever happened to you; the next minute, you hear a certain song or think of someone you love, and suddenly the spirit rises and you're feeling hopeful again, at least for the moment.

One day everything makes sense and you feel the presence of an all-loving God who has everything in control and every detail worked out. Other days, it feels like the ride is being run by a sadistic operator who takes pride in bringing you suffering. Strap on your seatbelt and hang on because you don't know where the ride is going to take you when you wake up in the morning.

Live like that from day to day and it can feel like your moods and emotional responses are at the mercy of whatever's happening around you. But what's really fascinating to me is seeing how the exact same things can have profoundly different effects on different people. What sends one person into a tizzy—like finding out they're losing their job—can charge up somebody else because they can't wait to try something new. Which says to me that the source of the tumult isn't in the circumstances themselves but rather how those circumstances are perceived by the gray matter between our ears.

"There is nothing either good or bad, but thinking makes it so," wrote Shakespeare, a man clearly well ahead of his time. Nearly four hundred years before the advent of modern cognitive psychology, the great bard understood the power of the thinking mind to warp and distort our perception of reality by labeling things as good or bad, happy or sad, awesome or sucky, and everything in between.

The truth is that reality itself, the stuff of this world, is neutral. It's a blank canvas, a tabula rasa. The mind paints onto that canvas all the meaning it has for us. That tree that fell on your brand-new car isn't trying to ruin your life. It's just a tree whose roots became diseased and could no longer withstand eighty-mile-an-hour winds from that nor'easter storm that moved up the coast. The cancer that killed Bob Marley at such a young age was tragic because it cut short a young life and an incredible talent. But the cancer was just doing what it's genetically programmed to do.

This road I'm walking now. That gorgeous sugar maple tree decked out in its fall finest. The Taco Bell sign I saw a couple of miles back. In and of themselves, all these things mean nothing. A visitor from another planet, seeing these things for the first time, would have no idea what they are. To him (it?), the Taco Bell sign would just be an object sticking up from the ground. But for me—someone who has driven on plenty of roads, who has seen plenty of sugar maple trees before, who has eaten more Taco Bell burritos than I would like to admit—for me, these things carry the meanings that I've loaded onto them over the years from past experiences.

"We see only the past," teaches A *Course in Miracles*, one of the handful of books I've read that I can truly claim to have changed my life. When I first read the book many years ago, at a dark time in my life, it brought home for me the many ways that the mind paints its own meanings onto the things it sees, hears, smells, and tastes. The mind is a label-stamping machine, much like the corporate marketing engines that painted all those signs that I saw while passing through Montgomeryville. The mind judges . . . interprets . . . categorizes . . . sees meanings in things that aren't there . . . frets and worries . . . strings events and circumstances into life stories that confirm beliefs we have of ourselves and of the world . . . all of which increases the likelihood that the circumstances will happen again.

## Early Lessons

I have spent a lot of time over the years pondering the ways of the mind, mainly because my own gave me so much trouble for so long. If I didn't get a grip on it, I would likely be in a cemetery somewhere right now instead of walking down this road.

Whereas the ways of the spirit revealed themselves early to me in my life, I needed to learn the ways of the mind through a painstaking, gut-wrenching combination of study and real-world experience. That experience came by necessity through suffering, which is always the best teacher.

Books and sages can point the way, but suffering makes the lessons sink in. You reach a point in your suffering where you realize that what you've been doing for so long isn't working and is never going to work, and you throw up your hands and begin to look for another way. That realization is the crack of light that can lead you out of the darkness to freedom.

For reasons I didn't fully understand until I was older, my mind set impossibly high standards for myself and the world around me. I could blame this on my father, who, it is true, did set a rather high bar for his children. He grew up on a dairy farm during the Depression where he learned the values of hard work and self-reliance, and he was eager to pass on his brand of fierce, rugged individualism to his kids. Not otherwise a literary man, he would go about the house reciting the lines of a Henry Wadsworth Longfellow poem that he had picked up somewhere in his youth:

> *Be not like dumb, driven cattle!*
> *Be a hero in the strife!*
> *For the soul is dead that slumbers,*
> *And things are not as they seem.*

With these words, my father threw down the gauntlet for his children. We had a choice in our lives: We could be cattle, or we could be heroes. Cattle are followers. They dumbly follow the cow in front of them, all the way to the slaughterhouse, or over the cliff, or wherever else the herd is going. Cows lie down in the face of a coming storm, waiting for direction, because that's all they know how to do.

Heroes, on the other hand, are leaders. They think for themselves and are not afraid of going their own way, even if that means going it alone. Heroes don't run away from their problems or lie down waiting for the storm to pass. They face their challenges with all the determination, intellect, and willpower they can muster. And they never give up.

Two different paths in life, my father challenged us. What are you going to be—a cow or a hero? A follower, or a leader? A conformist, or a trailblazer?

Another kid might have shrugged off these words as mere "Dad-isms." Not me. My impressionable adolescent mind, hungry for a place in the world, took my father's pronouncements to heart. It became my life's goal to achieve. To excel. To stand out from the crowd. To be a hero.

## At War with the Self

And so the pressure cooker of my life was switched on. For thirty years, from the time I was in high school and well into my forties, I pushed myself relentlessly to succeed. It was not enough that I get good grades; I had to get straight As. It was not enough that I wrote stories that entertained and moved people; I had to write serious literary novels that won awards and critical acclaim. It was not enough that I had a good life and enjoyed myself along the way; I had to make a difference in the world. I had to be a hero.

This is a tough way to live. When your mind demands that reality conform to your expectations of it, you're setting yourself up for a lot of stress and disappointment, and I got that in reams. When the books didn't come, when the awards and acclaim didn't come, when my seemingly perfect marriage went south, I pushed myself even harder. When all my self-induced stress plunged my sensitive nervous system into a clinical depression, my perfectionist mind demanded that I correct the faults that sucked me down into this black hole in the first place.

For years I was at war with myself, and that is a war that can never be won. The more I raged against the beast, the more ferociously he roared back. My moods were storms over which I had no control. The depressions and anxiety would descend on me seemingly out of the blue and shroud me in darkness for weeks and months at a time.

My mind made my life such a living hell that I took the ball out of its hands and gave it to someone else. Fed up with being miserable, I turned things over to my true self, my higher self—what Michael Singer in *The Untethered Soul* calls the observer. It's the "I" behind the thinking mind, the self that is able to calmly watch the ego go about its delusional thinking and even be a little amused by the whole thing.

To get to this point, though, I had to do a lot of work. One does not become a good manager of one's own personal ball club without a lot of training first. I became a student of psychology—namely, my own. I spent hundreds of hours on the therapist's couch talking through my fears and feelings. I read dozens on self-help books on depression, anxiety, cognitive behavioral therapy, positive psychology, nutrition, relaxation techniques, and all kinds of related topics. I meticulously catalogued my moment-to-moment thoughts and emotions. I wrote down and memorized new mental scripts for myself to replace the ones that had been running on autopilot since I was a kid.

Through this journey of inner work, I came to understand the profound connection between mind and body. I came to understand that every emotion is preceded by a thought, and every thought is preceded by a belief, and all beliefs are preceded by conditioning and early-life experiences—and that this whole cause-and-effect process happens on autopilot, below the level of our awareness. I came to understand that by becoming aware of this complex chain of stimulus-thought-belief-emotion, we can interrupt and change it, thereby changing the way we feel.

Most important, I came to understand that pessimism and negative thinking are not hardwired into us, that we are not victims of our genes, our circumstances, our anything. By training our mind, we can learn to be optimistic, to look at the glass of life as being half full, not half empty.

## Tricks of the Mind

Training anything, whether it's a mind or a dog, requires understanding how that thing works. Here's what I learned about the mind by studying my own admittedly messed-up one:

- The mind is an extremely powerful tool designed by nature for the purpose of performing tasks and getting things done.

- Give the mind a job to do and it will work relentlessly to achieve its mission. The more importance the mind attributes to its missions and goals, the more intensely it will work on achieving them, often to the exclusion of everything else.
- The mind responds equally well to conscious or unconscious commands. Conscious commands are those that you're aware of and verbalize. Unconscious commands are those you're not aware of, coming perhaps from underlying belief systems or unresolved past traumas. So, the mind can be working on something that you're not aware of until one day you see it magically delivered to your door.
- If your mind is not achieving what you want it to achieve, more than likely the commands you are giving it either aren't clear or are in conflict with something else you have asked it to do.
- As a task-driven instrument, the mind loves to-do lists. It's always creating lists and working on them. Finish one list and it starts another. The only time it rests is during sleep, and even then it is busy creating dreams where it hashes out all the fears it was unable to resolve during waking hours.
- For all its incredible powers of analysis and focus, the mind is curiously unable to filter out the word *not* in the instructions it is given. Instruct it to *not* make you depressed or anxious and it strips out the word *not* and proceeds to make you depressed and anxious—just as you instructed. Hence, it's important to state the instructions you give your mind in positive terms

of what you *want* rather than what you *don't want*—in other words, say, "I want to be more confident and self-assured," not "I don't want to feel anxious and insecure."

This last realization was huge for me in my own journey to peace. In working so hard to make myself feel better, in searching so intently for solutions to my anxiety and depression, I was actually making myself more depressed and anxious. My mind was manifesting the precise emotional states that I was instructing it to get me out of. But it was only doing what it was designed to do, which is all about control.

Control is the mind's modus operandi. It sees the world as a Darwinian fight to the death for limited resources, and sees its own role as maximizing the individual's odds of survival. Since (so the mind thinks) resources are scarce and likely to become more so in the future, the mind wants to find as many patches of grass as possible for the host to feed on, and put fences around them so that others don't try to take them away.

Which is where the ego comes in.

Being that the world is such a big, scary place and the self is so small and powerless, the mind feels a desperate need early on in life to carve out a defensible identity for itself. Hence, the importance of the ego, which is the mind's greatest creation and most protected treasure. The ego is the mind's way of making the self appear larger than it is—much as a blowfish does to fool bigger predators. The mind starts working on its ego identity early in life and continues carving away until the moment when the body gives its final breath, at which point the ego gives up the ghost as well.

The ego thinks it is the lord and master of the self. Every waking minute, it is giving the mind orders and instructions about what it wants, or what it thinks it wants. In reality, the ego is nothing but a projection, of no greater substance than that puffed-up blowfish; pop it with a pin and you wouldn't have enough meat to fry up for dinner. But the mind doesn't know that. The mind knows only that it has been given a command, and its job is to serve its master, even if its commands are in conflict with the deeper wants of the higher self.

## The Many Wants of the Ego

Unlike the mind, which, being but a tool, cannot want, the ego wants all the time. In fact, all the ego really *does* is want. It is a fickle master, and its wants are insatiable. It wants more money, more power, more status and influence, more achievement, more land, more fenced-off patches of grass. It wants all these things to make itself look bigger and more substantial, like that little blowfish swimming among the reeds.

The many wants of the ego are not the true wants and needs of the self. They are as fake as the masks people wear every day in a corporate environment. Nonetheless, the ego keeps churning out its to-do list of wants and desires, and the task-driven mind dutifully responds to those commands. Which is why the mind is always so busy. Not only must it meet the very real physical needs of the body; it must also satisfy the many needs and wants of the puffed-up ego.

Why is the ego-mind so needy? you may ask. If the many wants and desires of the ego are not real, where do they come from?

The answer, I've found, has to do with core beliefs. The house of the ego is built on a foundation of core beliefs: beliefs about the world, about the self, about other people, and lots of other things. These core beliefs form early in life based on the ego's warped perception of what's going on around it.

One of my early-formed core beliefs, for example, was that no one noticed me. I was the third of six children and thus suffered from middle-child syndrome. My siblings used to tease me that I was adopted, and there was a part of me that wanted to believe it, because that core belief gave me an identity in the world. From this core belief, in turn, arose my intense desire to achieve great things so that I could get the notice and attention I felt I deserved.

None of this stuff was real, of course. But that doesn't matter. What matters is that I believed it, because what we believe has a magical way of appearing in the circumstances of our lives thanks to the immense powers of the mind to create what it is seeking. The mind is an evidence-seeking magnet, and it attracts whatever confirms its beliefs about itself and the world. If we believe there is something fundamentally wrong with us, as I did for years of my life, then the mind will find evidence to support our brokenness. If we believe that people take advantage of us and treat us unfairly, the mind will find the evidence of life's unfairness. If we believe we are bad at managing money and fated to be poor all our lives, the mind will show us why this is so—and presto!—we will be poor.

Conversely, if we believe that we are healthy and whole, that life is generally pretty fair and full of abundance and blessings, then the mind will find evidence for that as well. We tend to get what we are looking for, and we see through the prism of our core beliefs. The more strongly held the belief, the greater the lengths the ego-mind will go to defend its illusions and prove them true. This is the case regardless of whether or not the belief is actually helpful or healthy to the self in its journey through life. It doesn't matter. The mind is simply serving the commands of its master the ego.

The mind does all these things to help navigate the self safely on the perilous journey through life. And all in all, it does a pretty amazing job. But there's a downside, and it's a big one. All the labeling, judging, and story-making adds weight and baggage to our journeys, turning the joyful flight of a butterfly into a laborious slog through mud.

It's the craziest damn thing, really, when you think about it. We are given this wonderful playground to walk through during our sojourn on this Earth, this awesome world of fluttering butterflies and babbling streams and majestic mountains and, for the most part, friendly people. If we're lucky, we have maybe eighty or ninety years to spend here. And what do we do? We load up that playground with lots of meanings, judgments, beliefs, and expectations, and life becomes no fun at all.

Such is the power of the ego-mind to spoil and soil our experience of life. The ego is so bent on defending and perpetuating its delusions that it is perfectly willing to make us miserable.

# The Spirit Connection Back to Joy

Fortunately, we have another creative force in our lives that we can tap into at any moment to take us back to peace and joy. The spirit is every bit as powerful as the mind in manifesting things in our lives, but it operates in completely different ways.

Whereas the mind operates on the basis of scarcity and exclusion, the spirit works from the principles of abundance and inclusion. It sees the world as an ever-flowing spring of unlimited, life-giving water that nourishes and feeds all living things. Whereas the mind is about control and striving, the spirit is all about surrender and release. The spirit understands that everything is connected and that what the mind perceives as separateness is really only the opposites that exist within all things.

When we are in the spirit, there is nothing to strive for because everything that is, was, and ever will be already exists right now in the present moment. If something feels missing—love, joy, peace, happiness, abundance—it's because some illusion held by the ego-mind has gotten in the way. To get to that river of abundance is a matter of letting go of whatever is blocking the flow.

We know we are in the spirit by how we feel. We feel happy. We feel joyful. We feel connected. We are fully engaged in whatever is going on around us and within us in the present moment. We are neither in the past nor the future, neither regretting something that's happened nor worrying about something that may happen. All fear and anxiety melt away. What is there to be afraid of when we contain everything?

I knew the truth of this intuitively as a child, when I lived every day in the spirit. But back then, I did not have awareness of how I was manifesting these feelings of peace and joy and connection. Meanwhile, my ego-mind was busily blowing itself up because of its many insecurities and warped perceptions of the world. Before I knew it, my ego-mind was in control, and the spirit was drowned out in all the mental noise. Life moved from a walk through a field of butterflies to a slog through routine and drudgery.

Self-understanding, combined with a daily practice of gratitude, is the road that takes us back to the spirit. It's not an easy hill to climb. There's a lot of work involved in getting there. The victory, however, is well worth the effort. When we gain that higher vantage point of awareness, we get to choose which path we want to take in our walk through life. Peace and happiness become a conscious choice. We move from being at the mercy of circumstances to being creators of our own fates.

When that happens, we get to worry a lot less. We can finally take Bob Marley's age-old advice:

*Don't worry . . . about a thing,*
*'Cause every little thing gonna be all right.*

# 9

# Dr. B. and the School of the Self

*Midway upon the journey of life, I found myself within a forest dark, for the straightforward pathway had been lost.*

—Dante, Inferno

The gleeful shouts of children bring me back to the scenes of my long walk home.

I'm passing a middle school that is letting out for the day. Shouting kids toting colorful backpacks pour out the side doors of the school building toward waiting cars and buses.

Ah, those easy, breezy days of school. I scratch my head when I hear people talk about how much they hated school when they were younger. I loved it. I loved high school. I loved college. Yeah, the tests and papers were a drag. But I enjoyed learning and being challenged. I knelt thirsty before the hydrant of knowledge, guzzling it down, never satiated.

It's amazing, though, considering all the years I spent in the classroom, how ill-prepared I was for life when I got out of school. I learned how to study and apply myself and write a well-organized paper. I learned how to do algebra and calculate the discounted value of a future stream of cash flows. I learned the Profession of Faith, the Stations of the Cross, and the stain of original sin that I carried with me when I was born into this world. But I learned precious little about the workings of the mind and how human beings are able to create either a heaven or hell of our lives by the way we think.

Shouldn't schools teach us this stuff? Instruct us on the fine art of manifesting what we want in life rather than what we don't want?

## The Art of Manifesting What We Want

Even that statement itself would have made no sense to me thirty years ago. Why would I even want to manifest what I do not want? That's crazy!

But it's not crazy. We human beings do it all the time. We not only regularly manifest things we don't want; we also manifest things that are bad or unhealthy for our bodies, our spirits, and our higher selves. Think of all the people who destroy themselves through drugs, drinking, smoking, and other self-destructive behaviors. These are all clear evidence of a self that isn't integrated, whose parts aren't working in unison for the greater interests of the whole.

I was on that path myself for years—not because of out-of-control behaviors, but ironically because my ego-mind was too much in control of my life, to the exclusion of my other parts. I didn't realize this was happening until it was nearly too late. I mean, it was obvious that something was terribly wrong. I was so crippled with anxiety and panic attacks that at one point I could barely leave my house. I thought the answer to my problems was to exercise more mental control, more discipline, more rule over the unruly states of my inner kingdom.

The more I did this, the worse I got. It was like being caught in a Chinese finger trap. The more you pull on either end in an attempt to free your hands, the tighter the grip becomes.

I got myself into this state, sad to say, because of ignorance. Anyone who says ignorance is bliss hasn't been through the hell of clinical depression. Having been there myself a number of times, I can say with certainty that ignorance is most definitely not bliss.

Knowledge is bliss. Understanding is bliss. Awareness is bliss. Bliss is what happens when we get all our disparate internal elements working in alignment with our innermost desires and spiritual purpose.

Bliss happens when we make the internal map visible, when we bring the entire apparatus of our internal manifesting machine—all our automatic triggers, levers, deep-held beliefs, traumas, sensitivities, doubts, and insecurities—out of the darkness into the light of conscious awareness.

Bliss is what happens when we take the wheel of our manifesting machine, rather than having it operate on autopilot. We gain the ability to manifest what we want rather than what we do not want.

Which is why, along with our diplomas, I believe they ought to hand us at graduation a cheat sheet of truths for the journey ahead. Call it "Secrets to Manifesting What You Want in Life." Something along these lines:

> *Remember, dear graduate, that you are not your body. You are not your mind. The fact that you can even think about your mind is proof that you are more than your mind.*
>
> *What you are, the "I" that you call yourself, is a unique blending of mind and spirit, contained temporarily in the form of a body and governed by a higher consciousness that knows intuitively what is best for you, if only you will listen.*
>
> *When these parts are working in unison, life can be an amazing journey filled with wonderful joys and abundance. Conversely, when these elements are in disharmony and working against one another, life can turn into a living hell on Earth.*
>
> *Which way you go is up to you.*
>
> *Commit to learning about yourself. There are vast worlds within you waiting to be discovered.*

*Find yourself a good shrink. A life guide, if you prefer. Dante needed Virgil, Luke Skywalker needed Yoda, the Karate Kid needed Mr. Miyagi. You'll need someone, too. But beware: There are many sophists out there who will lead you down false paths. Seek out the seekers, the truth-tellers, the inner warriors. You'll know them by the peace they exude.*

*Learn from the experience of others. There is nothing new under the sun. What you are going through, many others have gone through before.*

*Hang onto this cheat sheet and refer to it often. Though none of it makes sense right now to your eighteen-year-old brain, trust us when we say that you're going to need it someday.*

## Remembrance of a Doctor Visit

Speaking for myself, I know a cheat sheet like that would have helped me immensely in my walk through life. As it was, I needed to bumble my way through the brambles and nearly drive myself insane in the process.

In fact, thinking back on certain periods of my life, I believe I really was insane. It wasn't the type of insanity you see in books and movies, where people run around shouting profanities and tearing their hair out. But if insanity is defined as being out of touch with reality, I was there, or perilously close to it.

As I walk now on this beautiful October day humming Bob Marley, I recall a day back when my mind was so thick with fretting and worry that my mother took me to see our family doctor to figure out what was wrong with me. That morning, I had broken down crying at the breakfast table. I was twenty-one years old, in fine physical shape, but inside I was a mess. I couldn't sleep, had lost my appetite, my heart was racing constantly, and I couldn't stop my mind from spinning in circles like a dog chasing its tail.

At the time I was working my first job as a sportswriter for a weekly newspaper, but it wasn't what I wanted to be doing. I didn't want to be writing recaps of the local high school football team's big Friday win against its local rival. I wanted to be writing self-important novels that got reviewed in the *New York Times Book Review*. So commanded my ego-mind, which was firmly in charge of things at the time. It was putting immense pressure on me to get out of my small-town home and go to New York City, because I believed that's what young writers were supposed to do. Adding to the pressure cooker, my first romantic relationship had hit the rocks and I didn't know how to handle the tumult of emotions the breakup was creating within me.

I was keeping all this inside, trying to figure it out on my own, spinning my wheels deeper and deeper in the rut. I had cogitated myself into a state of nervous exhaustion, to the point where I could barely function. My mind, which had served me well enough up to now, had become my enemy. I couldn't make the simplest decisions. Thoughts had become arrows, tormenting me. I couldn't eat or sleep. Whenever I lay my head down on the pillow, a nameless terror gripped me.

So I called in sick from work and went with my mother to visit the family doctor. He was a young guy with glasses and a mustache and a rather dismissive way of dealing with the common complaints his patients brought to him every day. I described to him the symptoms I'd been having and told him I feared I was going crazy.

"You're not going crazy," he said, reaching out and rapping his knuckles against the wall. "You know this is a wall, don't you?"

I remember staring at the wall and not being able to answer. Yes, I knew I was looking at a wall, but I didn't know who the "I" was who was doing the looking. The "I" that I knew to be myself—whatever glued together my collective thoughts, feelings, experiences, interests, and desires—all those bindings had disintegrated, and I felt like I was walking through the world without my skin. Everything was too loud, too heavy, too much.

My parents, alarmed by the meltdown of their middle son, took me for an evaluation at a local mental-health center. The head of the practice, likely seeing what a long slog it was going to be with this kid, put me under the care of a freshly minted young psychologist with a hard-to-pronounce Italian last name. "Dr. B.," as he became known to me, was only about ten years older than I was, having recently graduated with a PhD in cognitive-behavioral psychology. I think I was one of his first patients as a new doctor. And he sure had his hands full with me.

## Working with Dr. B

Dr. B.'s first task was to get me settled down enough that we could talk about what the hell was going on inside me. Sitting in the quiet of his office, he taught me diaphragmatic breathing and progressive relaxation techniques. He gave me a tape to take home and do on my own. Being a good student and desperate to feel better, I diligently listened to the tape and did the exercises in my bedroom, in my car, on my lunch break at work, whenever I had a free moment.

After a few weeks, when I was settled down enough to be able to hold an intelligible conversation, Dr. B. began slowly to unpack the box of my psyche that had brought me to my current state. In twice-weekly sessions, we talked about my childhood, my home life, my time at college, my relationship with my girlfriend, and my grief over our breakup. We talked about my feelings, my fears, my beliefs about the world and myself.

For every sentence that came out of my mouth, Dr. B. had a question: Why did I think that? What evidence did I have for feeling that way? When I said I feared I would never have another girlfriend, he asked me if it was reasonable to think that, with all the girls in the world, I would never be able to find someone else who would want to be with me. When I said I couldn't do anything right, he got me to admit to the many things I had done successfully in my life, such as my sterling academic record at college. When I discounted those past successes by saying they didn't matter, he pressed me on what I considered success and whether it was realistic and productive to be beating myself up the way I was.

At the end of our forty-five-minute sessions, Dr. B. would give me homework to do. He had me read David Burns's book *Feeling Good: The New Mood Therapy*, a staple of cognitive-behavioral therapy. He had me do the exercises at home and keep a notebook tracking my emotional upsets and the thoughts that accompanied them. We talked about cognitive distortions: all-or-nothing thinking, overgeneralizations, catastrophic thinking, jumping to conclusions. He taught me how to catch myself when I was making these distortions in my thinking, to challenge those distorted thoughts and replace them with more realistic ones.

I was a year out of college but back in school, undergoing the most important education of my life. This was no innocuous elective course on "The Rise of the Antihero in Modern American Literature." This was life-or-death stuff. I was fighting just to get through the day and to keep my job. I was waging an inner war with a black beast that for some reason wanted to see me dead.

As Dr. B. dissected my thinking and rigid belief systems, I kept trying to bring our conversations back to the way I was feeling, the bizarre set of sensations I was experiencing on a daily basis. For every symptom, Dr. B. had a term.

"My head's fuzzy," I said. "I can't think right. It's like I'm walking through sludge."

"That's the depression."

"I feel like I'm looking down at myself. Like my eyes are detached from my body."

"That's part of the anxiety. It's called depersonalization."

"My thoughts hurt. I think something and it feels like an arrow shot through my gut."

"Your nervous system is sensitized from prolonged cogitation over these things you're worried about."

"I get hot flashes when I'm at work. I feel like I'm going to pass out. I think something's wrong with my heart."

"It's a panic attack. There's nothing wrong with your heart."

I didn't believe him. There had to be something physically wrong with me: a chemical imbalance, an overactive thyroid, a vitamin deficiency, something. I went for test after test. They all came back fine. I was fit as a fiddle.

"Do other people feel this way?" I asked.

"Lots of people feel this way. I see them every day in my office."

"I don't know of anyone."

"People generally don't like to talk about this sort of thing."

"Am I bipolar?" It was a term I had heard somewhere, and it scared me.

"No. Yours is a unipolar depression."

"How do you know?"

He explained the differences between unipolar and bipolar depressions. "You exhibit none of the symptoms of mania, like feelings of grandiosity or going out on wild spending sprees."

Dr. B. pulled from his shelf a thick blue book with the rather forbidding title of *Diagnostic and Statistical Manual of Mental Disorders*. He paged through it and pointed to the entry for major depressive disorder.

"This is what you have," he said. "Otherwise known as clinical depression."

He had me read it. All of the symptoms I had been feeling for months were listed there on the page, described in cold, clinical terms.

"Millions of people feel the way you do," he said. "It's an illness. Just like somebody with the flu can expect to feel feverish and congested, so you can expect to feel this way when you're depressed."

The feelings would fade over time, Dr. B. promised, as we got our arms around what was causing all the tumult within me. In the meantime, he said, I needed to accept the feelings, inconvenient as they were. Because fighting the feelings would only make them worse.

## Cognitive Dissonance

The weeks went by. The lessons continued.

There in Dr. B.'s office, we talked and talked and talked. One of the things we talked a lot about was stress: what it was, what caused it, the bad stuff it led to. Stress led to all kinds of ailments and illnesses, he related, and it started in the gray matter in our heads. Stress arises when we hold beliefs and values that conflict with one another. *Cognitive dissonance* was the term he used for it.

"And you, Jim," he said, leaning toward me and looking me in the eye, "you do not like conflict. You like things to be black and white. Perfect. Packaged up in a nice square box and tied with a bow. And unfortunately, that is not the real world. The real world is messy."

What I was going through right now, the doctor explained, was a bit of an existential crisis. It happened a lot with young people when they come out of the structured, orderly world of school and find out that life is not a classroom with a defined syllabus and a test at the end of the semester.

But there was good news in all this, the young doctor reassured me. The distress I was feeling was an indication that a reordering process was underway inside of me. Though it felt awful, I shouldn't be afraid of it.

"Chaos," he said, "is the first step toward reorganization."

If reorganization was what this was, then all I knew was that it seemed to be taking a godawful long time to happen.

Six months had passed since my meltdown at the kitchen table and I was still struggling to make it through the day. At times, it felt like my twice-weekly therapy sessions with Dr. B. were all I was hanging onto. At the beginning of each session, he had me fill out a brief questionnaire to show where I was on the depression scale. My scores weren't budging. Since, as a psychologist, Dr. B. could not prescribe medication, he referred me to a psychiatrist who put me on meds for anxiety and depression. All the pills seemed to do was make me sleepy.

I wanted to crawl out of my skin like a shedding snake, but there was no escape. The months dragged on with no relief. The pain was unremitting. Some days, my despair was so awful, all I did in Dr. B.'s office was cry. I cried rivers of tears. I cried until I didn't think I had any more tears inside me, and then I cried some more. I felt like my guts were being ripped out through my throat.

"Having a bad day?" Dr. B. would ask me somberly when I walked into his office with tears in my eyes.

"I can't do this anymore," I would say.

"Yes, you can."

"I can't. It's unbearable."

"It's painful, yes," he came back. "It's inconvenient. But it's bearable. You just need to hang in there and in time, you will feel better."

"How do you know for sure?" I challenged him. I wanted assurances. I wanted guarantees.

"No depression lasts forever," he replied confidently.

"How do you know? Have you ever been through this before?"

He shook his head. "Not personally, no. But why is that important?"

"Because if you've been through it yourself, you would know," I said.

"If you have a broken leg," Dr. B. replied calmly, "would you need a surgeon who'd had a broken leg himself in order to operate and make you better?"

Logic. Rationality. Challenging the basis of unquestioned beliefs and assumptions. Delving beneath the surface of distorted thinking. With Dr. B. as my guide, I was learning to discipline my mind, my thinking, my perceptions. But though much of what he said made sense to my rational mind, it wasn't doing a thing to change my feelings. By now, I'd been in therapy for more than a year and I still felt awful. Why wasn't I getting better? Cognitive-behavioral therapy was supposed to work quickly, more quickly than the old-school Freudian analysis methods. Why wasn't it working for me? I must be hopeless.

With every month that passed without relief, the feeling that I was a hopeless case built inside of me. I went for more tests, all of which came back normal. The psychiatrist prescribed new meds to try to break through my treatment-resistant depression. Nothing made a dent in my suffering.

For his part, Dr. B. insisted there was nothing physically wrong with me and that I wasn't going to find an answer in pharmacology. I just needed to hang on, keep plugging away at it, keep working on my thinking, and in time I would feel better.

# Return to Life

He was right. I did get better, although it took me a lot longer than I suspect even Dr. B. believed it would. After two years of therapy, I started experiencing some short windows of relief. Week by week, those windows expanded until, after another six months or so, I was able to cut down on our twice-weekly sessions, which was good because I was spending half of my small salary at the newspaper on doctor visits.

Three years after my meltdown at the kitchen table, I left my small-town newspaper job and began a graduate-level creative-writing program in Philadelphia. I was twenty-five years old and living on my own for the first time. My anxiety levels were off the charts, and half the time I felt like I was walking around in a fog, but at least the darkness of depression had receded. Soon after graduating from the two-year program, I began working for the company. Two years after that, I met my future wife and we got married.

Light and happiness had returned to my life. I got off all the meds that weren't helping me anyway. I stopped my weekly visits with Dr. B.

Fifteen years went by. I thought I was better. I thought I had learned the lessons I needed to learn to never again go back down into that pit of depression. I thought I had mastered my unruly mind and defeated the black beast once and for all, and that it would never rear its ugly hide in my life again.

I was wrong. My education was far from over. The hardest lessons were still to come.

# 10

# The Splinter of Discontent

*The most common form of despair is not being who you are.*

—Søren Kierkegaard

Something is going on up ahead on the road. A line crew is out replacing an electric utility pole. The old creosote-soaked pole has splintered in the middle and the guys are working on connecting power to a brand-new shiny pole planted next to the old one.

My eyes go to a yellow-hatted guy riding the service bucket high at the end of service truck's boom. Man, that's a job I would not want. The current flowing through those electric lines could fry a person like a mosquito in a bug zapper, and knowing my propensity for accidents, I would probably touch the wrong wire and that, as they say, would be that.

Though I am not a fan of utility companies in general, I really admire the service and maintenance people who work for those firms. What they do to restore power in short order after a storm is nothing short of miraculous. I wouldn't have a clue how to do their jobs. Ask me to drill a hole or saw a board or put a molly bolt in the wall and I can handle it. Not electrical—I just don't have a head for that kind of thing. As a kid, my eyes would glaze over whenever my electrical engineer father tried to explain how a closed circuit works and the role of a ground wire in an electrical outlet. He might as well have been speaking Pennsylvania Dutch (which he would do sometimes).

In truth, I've always been a bit afraid of electricity, stemming from the time when, as a young boy, I stuck a butter knife into a wall socket of our old farmhouse and got a jolt that sent me flying backwards across the room. I suppose it's perfect symmetry, then, that thirty-some years later I would have to resort to electricity in a desperate attempt to find healing. After all, we tend to attract that which we fear and resist most.

## Memories of a Dark Period

As I walk past the line crew and continue up the road, I think back on that terrible period in my forties, when I had to take a leave of absence from work to have twelve rounds of electroshock therapy in a desperate attempt to break through my years-long depressive fog. Did it really happen? Was I really that lost to myself, lost to my kids, lost to the world? Or is what I'm remembering just the remnants of a horrible dream concocted by my overactive imagination?

But I know it wasn't just a dream. It really did happen. I really was that bad off. I have records of it. My folks remember it. I remember them driving me to the hospital for the treatments. I remember clearly seeing my mother blow me a kiss from the door as I was being wheeled into the staging room to be given the anesthetic. I remember the cold wet gel being applied to my temples for the electrodes. I remember lying in the bed afterward, feeling lighter in my head but not much else.

Still, it's hard to grasp. I mean, here I am out walking on this gorgeous fall day and, aside from being stressed out about losing my job, I feel fine. Anyone who talked to me would think I am perfectly normal. Which I am, depending on how you define "normal." I mean, I own a house. I have a mortgage. I pay taxes. I pay my bills on time and have an excellent credit score. I have three degrees. I am a good father. I hold down a highly responsible job for a multibillion-dollar company. Aside from that two-month leave of absence in my mid-forties, I have been working continuously for more than thirty years and am known to be a highly reliable worker and employee.

These aren't the attributes of a person who is out of touch with reality. But there's no question that I was out of touch with things during that dark period when my marriage was falling apart. I had gotten myself so wrapped around the axle of my troubles that my system had ground to a halt. It just goes to show what a labyrinth the ego-mind can create for itself when left to its own devices.

But the equally amazing thing is that today, more than ten years on, I'm able to look back at that dark period of my life and smile at the folly of it all. Which truly shows what the higher self can do to lead a person back from the deepest, darkest circles of hell to a place of light, peace, and abundance.

It is possible.

I know it's possible because I've lived it.

## The Fissure of Deepening Unhappiness

Electroshock therapy has gotten a bum rap in the public mind from the way it's been portrayed over the years in literature and movies. Think *One Flew Over the Cuckoo's Nest*, where the incorrigible Randle McMurphy (played by Jack Nicholson in the film version) is forcibly sent to the "shock shop" for bad behavior.

In truth, few cases of electroconvulsive therapy (ECT) are done involuntarily, and the treatment today is done safely and painlessly in hospitals while the patient is under anesthesia. Lots of famous people have reportedly had it: Judy Garland, Lou Reed, Tammy Wynette, Dick Cavett. ECT works by inducing a seizure in the brain, which has been found to be effective in relieving many of the symptoms of serious mental and emotional illnesses. For many, the treatment has allowed them to break out of the cycle of their illness and get back on the road to health.

Still, one doesn't arrive lightly at a place of undergoing ECT. It's a last-resort treatment for incalcitrant depression and other severe mental-health conditions, administered when nothing else has worked. ECT is not intended to cure those conditions but rather to provide temporary relief. Maybe a few months. Maybe just a few weeks. Everyone is different.

That's how I came to find myself lying on a hospital bed having seventy volts of current pulsed through my brain to induce a seizure intended to make me feel better. I was like that telephone pole back along the road: broken, splintered in half by a structural fissure revealed by the weight of an enormous load of stress. And it all began with a tiny splinter that I ignored because I didn't want to deal with it.

That splinter was my unhappiness with my marriage. Early on in the marriage, I became aware of a little voice of doubt within me that said maybe I had jumped the gun too quickly, that the relationship had issues, that my wife and I hadn't dated long enough to really get to know each other. But I swatted away the doubts, telling myself I was being unrealistic about my expectations for the marriage and the relationship. Besides, I wanted to be married. After the turmoil I had gone through in my early twenties, I wanted stability and normalcy.

As the years went on and the children came along, the issues thickened: communication issues, compatibility issues, lack of shared interests and goals. Like a lot of other people in unhappy marriages, we ignored them. We were busy, after all. My wife had quit her job to be a stay-at-home mom with our three young boys. I was moving up in my career at the company and working long hours. Our lives were crammed with things to do from the time we got up in the morning to the time we lay down our heads at night.

Beneath the surface of all that busyness, however, my unhappiness was growing. Though my wife and I didn't argue a lot, there was a current of unspoken conflict and negativity running through our marriage. I longed for a deeper emotional connection. I'm sure she did, too. For someone like me, with my propensity to feel things deeply, this was not healthy.

One day while on a business trip in San Francisco, I met a woman I was attracted to. The woman—let's call her Chrissy—was pretty and smart and bubbling over with positive energy. We sat next to each other during the conference and later went to dinner with a group of others at Fisherman's Wharf. I felt an instant connection to her. I was able to talk to her in a way I couldn't with my wife. We spoke about our work, our careers, our love of books and reading. Chrissy was engaged to be married in a couple months, but I sensed she was not particularly wild about her fiancé. I'm sure she could sense my underlying dissatisfaction with my marriage as well.

After dinner we made the long walk back to the hotel on Nob Hill, stopping for ice cream along the way. As we walked, I remember feeling alive in a way I hadn't felt in years. When we got back to the hotel, Chrissy gave me a look that indicated she was interested in something more. But I couldn't do it. I was married, even if she wasn't yet. I had made a vow, and keeping vows is important to me.

She went to her room and I went to mine. The next day we flew out—Chrissy back to Illinois where she lived, me home to Pennsylvania. We never saw each other in person again, but we stayed in touch. We would talk on the phone every week, sometimes every couple of days. She had gotten married and would talk obliquely about her new husband and their new life together. Mostly, we talked about work and books and our life goals and interests. I sent her pictures of my three sons. She sent pictures of her dog. We even exchanged books through the mail, our own private book club.

With every conversation, our emotional connection deepened. I would share with Chrissy things I didn't feel I could share with my wife. This went on for years. It was nuts. We were a thousand miles away from each other, both of us married, but growing steadily closer. What was I thinking? What was she thinking? We were both playing with fire.

## Tossed into Turmoil

Then, one day—this was after six years of speaking regularly by phone—Chrissy informed me that she and her husband were divorcing. She'd had doubts about the relationship for a long time and had given it a good try, but she and her husband just couldn't make the marriage work. She had left him and moved into a place of her own.

The news threw me into turmoil. She and I had been playing a fantasy game that was all very nice and safe because we were both married and living a thousand miles apart. But now the safety rails were off. The game wasn't theoretical any longer. This married woman whom I'd only met once and hadn't seen again in six years was now available. And I . . . was not.

Chrissy had made her move. Now it was my turn. It was time to get off this fence I'd been sitting on for too long.

But unlike her, I had children. Yes, I was deeply unhappy in my marriage, but the thought of breaking up my family sent shock waves of anxiety through me. I loved my boys deeply. How could I leave them? What I was contemplating clashed with my deepest values. Divorce? That kind of thing happened to other people. My parents had been married for fifty years. That's what I wanted for myself, for my kids.

Talk about cognitive dissonance: I was in the thick of it. Back and forth went the debate in my head:

It's *now or never.*
*But the kids.*
*The kids will be all right.*
*I can't leave.*
*You'll lose her if you don't move now.*
*No, I can't.*

Leave. Don't leave. Everything I had learned since my first meltdown twenty years ago went out the window. I was ruminating myself back into a ditch again. I fought desperately to counter the rising tide of darkness within by tracking my irrational thoughts and countering them with positive self-talk, but the more I fought, the worse I felt. I couldn't eat, couldn't sleep, couldn't rest. Dark thoughts circled my mind day and night like scavenging vultures. As soon as I sat or lay down, they would swoop down to torment me. I was having trouble concentrating at work. Panic attacks would wash over me during meetings and I would sneak off to the nearest bathroom to splash cold water on my face.

Get it together, Jim, I would admonish myself in the mirror.

*You remember that dark place.*

*You can't allow yourself to go back there.*

With every flash of panic, every shot of adrenaline and cortisol, my inner chemistry was changing. The black beast was stirring.

One night, a few weeks after Chrissy told me the news of her separation, I lay in bed next to my sleeping wife in our second-floor bedroom, unable to sleep. Again. My nightshirt was drenched with sweat, as was the sheet under me. I glanced at the clock—two in the morning. In another few hours I would need to get up for work. How would I be able to make it through another day in the office without sleep?

The thought caused more hot panic to flush through my system. I got up and made my way downstairs. I drank a glass of warm milk, hoping it would make me sleepy, but it did nothing. My heart was racing, my mind spinning like a bingo drum tossing dark thoughts, and the one thought that kept coming to the top of the barrel was a disturbing one:

*Kill yourself.*

*Get one of your guns.*

*Do it.*

I thought of my hunting rifles locked away in the cabinet in the next room. No! my rational voice shouted back. *Think of your kids! They're sleeping on the floor above you.*

But the demon voice was insistent:

*Your rifle.*

*Go get it.*

*Do it.*

I knew this demon. It was the black bear. It had been nearly twenty years since I'd heard its voice. I thought it was dead. I thought I'd killed him forever. But I hadn't. The bear was back again and raging—

*Get it.*

*Do it!*

Back and forth went the battle: demon voice versus voice of rationality. The demon voice was so strong. So insistent. I feared it. I feared the strength of the bear. What if my will-power wasn't strong enough to ward it off? What if I lost control and heeded the demon voice? I pictured myself getting my rifle out of the case in the next room, loading it, holding it against my head.

In full-blown panic attack, I got in the car and drove myself to the hospital.

## Back on the Roller Coaster

The wonderful nurses and doctors who staff hospital emergency rooms are very good at treating broken arms and wounds and other such outwardly visible medical conditions. But they're not as well equipped to helping people suffering from mental-health and emotional issues.

The ER nurse led me to a table and took my pulse and blood pressure. Then the attending doctor came in and listened to my tale of woe.

"Well, your vitals look good," he said. "We could do some tests but I don't think it's anything physical. Do you have a history of depression?"

"Yes," I admitted.

"Are you taking any medications for your depression?"

I shook my head no.

"Do you have a psychologist or psychiatrist?"

"Not at the moment," I told him.

"Do you need the name of someone?"

"I have someone I can call," I replied, thinking of Dr. B.

The doctor shook his head. "I'd suggest getting in touch with them right away and get a prescription for an antidepressant. It will take a few weeks to kick in, but it should help you."

A *few weeks*? I remember thinking. I wasn't sure how I was going to make it through the next few minutes, let alone the next few weeks.

"Do you feel you're going to hurt yourself if we let you out of here?" the doctor asked me.

I wasn't sure how to answer this. My rational mind said no. But I didn't trust the demon voice within me. It was quieter at the moment as I sat on this hospital bed, but I wasn't sure what would happen when I walked out of the emergency room.

"I don't know," I said. "I don't think so."

The doctor scratched his head puzzledly. "Well, we'll give you something for the anxiety, but there's not much more we can do for you here except watch you."

I ended up spending four hours in the emergency room before being released to the care of my parents, who drove me back to the home that I was so conflicted about.

And so began four years on the roller coaster.

I went back to seeing Dr. B. at his office, where I'd spent so much time in the past. It had been ten years since I'd seen him and we had a lot of catching up to do: my life, my work, my family. I told him about my long-simmering doubts about my marriage and about the phone relationship I'd been having with Chrissy.

"This other woman is a distraction," he told me. "You need to work on your relationship with your wife. That has to be your focus."

Soon after, I spoke with Chrissy over the phone and broke off our platonic relationship. I never spoke with her again. My wife and I began counseling. We started talking more. We recommitted to each other and our marriage.

For the next year or so, things were a little better. In addition to Dr. B., I was seeing a psychiatrist, who had me on an antidepressant as well as an anxiety medication. The pills helped even out my moods so that I was able to work. My wife was supportive of me and what I was going through and even bought me a self-help program for overcoming depression and anxiety. We worked on the practices together. We read inspirational books and shared passages with each other.

But then, at the end of the year, I crashed again. The pills stopped working and I plunged back into darkness. At Christmas I was so bad off that I voluntarily checked into a local mental-health clinic. I had never been to a behavioral clinic before, and even in the state I was in, it didn't take me long to figure out that this place wasn't going to do anything for me. I spent a few days wandering the halls with other lost souls, and on New Year's Day, I was released and sent home to continue my roller-coaster ride.

## Visits with the Queen of Scripts

With the holidays over, I went back to work, where I struggled mightily to hold it together. In the wake of the dot-com bubble, business was in the tank and the company was restructuring yet again in an attempt to turn things around. A new CEO had come onboard and there was a lot to do. I was right in the thick of it: telling our turnaround story to Wall Street analysts, answering questions from investors, managing a team of people. On top of my day-to-day responsibilities, I was going to night school, trying to finish up my MBA.

They were long days, and I fought to get through every minute. My brain was enveloped in a dense, black sludge and it took a monumental amount of willpower to tackle even the simplest of tasks. I felt like my skin had melted away and I was walking around with my nerves exposed to the world. Everything was too loud, too much. I didn't want to have to interact with anyone and I hid away in my office as much as I could, which isn't easy to do when you're working a high-profile job on a corporate campus with thousands of other people.

Most of all, I didn't want people around the office to find out what I was going through. I knew that if someone noticed my distress and asked me what was wrong, I would break down in tears, and I couldn't have that. So each morning,

I put on my stoic game face and went to the office for another day of pretending to have it together, all the while fighting to keep the façade from crumbling. Sometimes I would be sitting in an important meeting in the conference room when suddenly I would feel the tears welling in my eyes, and I'd slip off to the bathroom to sit in the stall and cry.

It felt much like what I had gone through twenty years ago when I worked at the newspaper after college, except now there were real stakes involved. I was not a kid anymore. I was forty-three years old with a family and financial responsibilities. I could not afford to lose my job, my salary, my benefits.

Desperate for relief, I went back to the psychiatrist in search of a medication that would help me. She saw patients in rapid-fire ten-minute intervals in her whitewashed medical office. I was convinced that there was a physical element to my depression—a chemical imbalance of some sort—that could be corrected with the right medication, and the doctor was more than happy to oblige me in my search. She was the queen of scripts. In the months to come, she wrote prescription after prescription for antidepressants. She titrated the dosages up and down, trying to find the level that would work for me. When one antidepressant didn't work, she tried another. Selective serotonin reuptake inhibitors; serotonin-norepinephrine reuptake inhibitors; monoamine oxidase inhibitors; tricyclics; atypicals: I tried them all.

I couldn't tell you how these different classes of antidepressants work and what makes them different from one another. But I can tell you this: They cause some nasty side effects. Some made me feel nauseated. Others made me dizzy and light-headed. A few made me so anxious, I wanted to crawl out of my skin. To counteract the anxiety, the psychiatrist put me on anti-anxiety meds. To increase the effectiveness of the antidepressants, she prescribed other meds: antipsychotics, anticonvulsants, antiseizure meds. Combination therapy, she called this. It was a standard approach for treatment-resistant depression, which was what she said I had. It happened for twenty to thirty percent of people with depression. Lucky me. But we would find something, she assured me; there were a lot of medications out there. We just had to find one that worked.

My head was swimming in a cocktail of chemicals. I didn't know what was up or down. I walked zombie-like through my days, doing my best to get my work done, to survive. None of the meds was making a difference in cutting through the sludge in my head. All they did was tame the demon voice inside me that wanted me dead. A good day was when the black bear wasn't raging wild inside me. A bad day was when the beast got fed up with being sedated and went on a rampage, ripping at my insides with its razor-sharp claws. I was firmly in the beast's grip and it wouldn't let go. For his part, Dr. B. didn't think medication was the answer. I was seeing him twice a week in his office, spending a small fortune in the process, and when I would tell him about the latest script the psychiatrist had written for me, invariably he would grimace and shake his head.

"Jim," he would say to me, "I really don't believe you're going to feel better until you resolve the situation with your marriage."

My unhappiness in the marriage was the splinter in my hide, he told me. It had been festering for a long time. He reminded me of my doubts early on about the marriage, going back to my honeymoon night. Then he asked me a question I had not thought much about.

"Why did you get married?"

"Because I wanted to," I replied.

"Do you still want to be married?"

The question hit me at the core. What did it matter what I wanted? I was married and I took my vows seriously. "I don't know," I replied.

"I think you do know."

"I don't want to hurt my kids."

Cognitive dissonance. A clash of values versus the hard surfaces of reality. Dr. B. nodded grimly. He understood the pickle I was in. He could not tell me what to do; it had to be my decision. And I was unable to choose.

## In the Grip of the Black Beast

Depression is often described as a whole-body illness. It's an illness that affects mind, body, and spirit alike. It affects your thinking, your moods, your health. It causes all sorts of unexplainable aches and pains. It takes away your ability to feel pleasure. It saps you of your stamina and strength.

What makes depression doubly hard to manage is that when you're in the arms of the black beast, the very instrument that you need most to escape its grip—your mind—is itself clouded. Because your thinking is fuzzy, you're not able to see your circumstances clearly and figure a logical way out of them. It's like being lost in the woods with a malfunctioning compass.

That's where I was at for those lost years while my marriage was breaking apart. I was so lost in the trees of my feelings that I could not see the bigger picture. Years of stressing about my circumstances had put my sensitive system into a state of nervous overload. And at the root of it all was the festering splinter in my hide that I could not summon the will to pull out because doing so would violate everything I believed about the importance of honoring my vows and commitments.

My values and beliefs were not real, but they were literally making me sick.

It seemed to me back then that if only I could get myself better, I would be able to think clearly enough to make the decisions I needed to make in my life. I went about this mission in a methodical fashion that would have made my engineer father proud.

I dutifully took my meds.

I bought dozens of self-help books and did the exercises.

I reread all the cognitive psychology books that I had read back in my twenties, retraining myself on the basics of cognitive-behavioral therapy.

I worked hard—very hard—to track my negative thoughts, note any distortions, and replace them with more realistic, positive thoughts and affirmations. I memorized those affirmations and went through the day reciting them to myself:

I am happy.
I am healthy.
I am strong.
I am calm and peaceful.
I love my wife and kids.
I am blessed with my wonderful family.

I even went so far as to stick Post-it notes on the walls at my home and at the office, reminding myself of these affirmations. But the affirmations felt false to me. I wasn't happy. I wasn't calm and peaceful. I didn't feel strong or powerful or blessed.

The demon voice of the beast knew I was faking it and ridiculed me:

*You have everything, Jim!*
*Why can't you just be happy?*
*What's the matter with you?*
*You're hopeless!*

## A Year and a Half in Hell

The black months stretched on. I was popping pills like pharmacological popcorn to get my system into some kind of equilibrium. Over a period of a year and a half, I tried close to twenty different medications in an effort to regain my equilibrium before the psychiatrist finally threw up her hands.

"I don't know what else to give you," she admitted one day in her office after the failure of yet another pill combination. "We've tried everything."

This was not making me feel any better.

The doctor looked at me. I could see the exasperation in her face, hear it in her voice.

"Have you tried hypnosis? she asked.

It was an offhand suggestion, but strangely, it gave me hope.

Could hypnosis work? If traditional approaches were not working for me, were there alternative therapies out there that could cut through the fog of my depression?

And so began a yearlong search for a magical elixir that could help me.

I tried hypnosis.

I tried acupuncture.

I tried vitamin therapy and colon cleansing.

I tried Reiki and energy therapy.

I tried homeopathy, aromatherapy, massage therapy.

I shelled out a couple of grand on a pricey meditation program that promised to make me a master meditator in a fraction of the time as the most-practiced yogi. Every morning, I sat for an hour with headphones listening to CDs that piped recorded binaural beats into my ears, taking me to ever-deeper levels of inner tranquility. The daily meditations provided a much-needed respite in my dark days, but when the hour was over, I was back to the reality of a troubled marriage and a conundrum I could not seem to find my way out of.

Deeper and deeper into the dark web I went in search of something that could help me. There are all kinds of people out there selling all kinds of homespun treatments if you look hard enough. I found a local woman who advertised tinctures for treating depression and other emotional ailments. I drove to her home and stepped through a cloth-draped door into her treatment room, where tincture bottles were held in a dispenser display. The woman listened as I described my symptoms and picked out a tincture. I drank it down, and waited. Nothing. She handed me a second bottle. The tincture tasted like flavored tea.

When I told her I felt nothing, the potion lady looked puzzled. I visited her twice, paid a hundred bucks, and never went back.

Soon after, I signed up for an experimental trial evaluating the effectiveness of transcranial magnetic stimulation (TMS) for treating treatment-resistant depression. Every week, I drove down the Schuylkill Expressway to the University of Pennsylvania to sit in a chair for thirty minutes with a cap on my head as the TMS machine clicked like a woodpecker hammering on a hollow tree. I felt nothing. After six weeks, I was told that it had all been a placebo—no wonder I hadn't felt anything—and I was now being moved to the active phase of the trial. So I sat for another six weeks as the machine delivered magnetic pulses into my skull. The pulses stung, but otherwise did nothing for me.

With every alternative therapy that failed, I sank deeper and deeper in despair. Nothing was working.

I truly was hopeless.

## The Therapy of Last Resort

Such was my state of mind when, in the spring of 2005, I took a two-month leave of absence from work and agreed to undergo electroconvulsive therapy.

I was in enough command of my faculties that I was deemed fit by my doctors to give my own informed consent to the procedure. Since my wife was busy with our kids, my parents drove me to the twice-weekly procedures at the outpatient center of the local hospital, where I was put in a bed, given an IV, and wheeled into the staging room.

As much as I would like to forget that entire experience, there are two things I am certain I will always remember. One was seeing my mother standing in the doorway, blowing me a kiss before the door was closed. The other memory was that I was not alone in this room. There were six or seven other beds with people lying on them. I remember seeing an older man, a middle-aged woman, a young woman about the same age as I was. As I was brought into the room, she looked over at me and gave me a weak smile. I felt a kinship with these people. They were all lost souls like me, lost in what-ever affliction had put them in those beds.

One by one, the team of nurses came to attend to us. I watched as the young woman next to me was wheeled out of the room. When she came back, ten minutes later, she was asleep but otherwise looked no different.

The nurse team came up to me.
"Your turn," the lead nurse said. The nurse looked down at me. She had a kind face. Kind eyes. "It's going to be all right," she said.

In the treatment room, a cold gel was smeared on my forehead.

"Okay, now it's off to sleep for you," she said.
I felt the anesthesia numbing my senses. Someone was putting soft-cup electrodes on either side of my temples. Then I was out.

When I woke up fifteen minutes later, I was back in the staging room, with the others. I felt lighter, as if I'd just had a really good laugh. The kind-eyed nurse came up to me. I remembered her. I remembered everything.

"How do you feel?" she asked.

"Okay," I said.

I did this twice a week for six weeks, for a total of twelve treatments. Statistically speaking, ECT is a highly effective therapy for treatment-resistant depression, leading in improvement in 70 to 90 percent of cases. Unfortunately, the improvements generally do not stick, and that was the case for me. I felt somewhat better, enough to go back to work, but after a couple of months, the benefits wore off and I was back in the grips of the beast.

## Pulling the Splinter

That's when things really started to get bad at home. My wife was at wit's end with me. The two of us had given up on counseling since it wasn't working, and having let go of any artifice that this marriage could be healed, we began fighting. The arguments would start first thing in the morning and continue as soon as I stepped back in the door of the house after work. The house was filled with tension.

Later that year, she approached me and said she wanted a divorce. I remember feeling immense relief at getting this news. It took off my shoulders the burden of making a decision that I was unable to make myself. We both hired lawyers. She wanted me out of the house. On the advice of my lawyer and my family, I refused. How could I abandon my kids? I moved into the spare bedroom. We were enemies living under the same roof, shooting at each other from across the hall. This went on for six awful months until an accident broke the stalemate. While out skiing with my brother, I broke my left leg and needed surgery. Unable to care for myself in a cast and crutches, I went to live with my sister and brother-in-law for a couple of months until I was able to move into a rental townhouse.

I was on my own again. I had plates in my legs, a muddled head, shredded nerves, and a drained bank account from all my medical and lawyer bills.

But I was out of the house. I had pulled, albeit reluctantly, the long-festering splinter of discontent from my flesh.

I could begin my healing.

# 11

# Mystic Pizza, Magic Oatmeal

*I have always been delighted at the prospect of a new day, a fresh try, one more start, with perhaps a bit of magic waiting somewhere behind the morning.*

—J. B. Priestley

My stomach gives a growl, reminding me that I haven't eaten lunch. All this walking and cogitating on an empty tank has left me famished. I really need to eat something.

Up ahead I spot a sign for Spatola's Pizza. A slice of pizza would go down really well right now, so I make a beeline toward the place and step inside, which is when I discover that I have something else to worry about.

I don't have any money with me. My wallet, I remember, is locked in the glove compartment of my car, which is parked back at the office. I often leave my wallet in my car since I don't need it during the day and don't want to carry it around with me at the office.

God, however, provides. I dig in my right pocket and discover a couple of rumpled dollar bills as well as some change left over from breakfast at the cafeteria that morning.

"How much is a slice?" I ask the teenage girl behind the counter.

"Two and a quarter," she replies.

Not cheap, but I'm hungry. "Perfect," I say.

I hand her the bills along with a couple of quarters, and so a transaction is made.

## Gratitude: The Path to the Spirit

Back on the road, I nibble on the pizza while taking in the rainbow colors of the fall day. Maybe it's just because I'm so hungry, but the warmed-up slice of pizza tastes fantastic. It might be the best pizza I've ever had. Being that I only have one slice and another ten miles still to go on my walk home, I eat it slowly, savoring each bite, while mulling over the explosion of flavors each bite brings into my mouth. Silently, I give thanks for the food and the nourishment and for being alive on a day like this, in all its glory.

The surest path to the spirit, I have found, is through gratitude. Appreciation for the little things leads to appreciation for the big things, and the whole chain leads to joy and happiness. It works like magic.

It took me a long time to discover this magical link. The first time I fell into the pit of clinical depression in my early twenties, I thought the way to get out was through mastery of my mind.

Though all that cognitive work helped me uncover unrealistic ways of thinking that were contributing to my depression, it wasn't enough to bring me to consistent levels of peace, joy, and happiness. It wasn't enough because I was looking for the solution in the mind itself. The mind was both patient and doctor. I was approaching the problem through the framework of the ego-mind's way of solving problems, not even realizing that there was another way.

And so, when I fell back into the dark pit in my forties while my marriage was falling apart, my mind went back into fix-it mode, believing there were still things I hadn't learned. I was determined to kill the beast inside me that kept dragging me down into the swamp. The harder I fought against it, the worse I felt.

It was only when I gave up the fight and surrendered to the spirit that I was able to claw my way back into the light. The process happened almost magically for me when I began to actively look for, notice, and give thanks for every blessing in my life, no matter how seemingly small.

The fact is, there are no small blessings. They are all portals to the spirit. Every time we give thanks for something, we step like the child Lucy through the wardrobe into the magical land of the spirit. The more blessings we look for, the more we see. The more we see, the more we appreciate. The more we appreciate, the better we feel.

Like magic.

# A Magical Bowl of Quaker Oats

My portal to the spirit was a hot bowl of Quaker oatmeal.

I was in my mid-forties, newly separated and living on my own in the rental townhouse. This was a few months after I had broken my leg in the skiing accident. The cast was off, but I was still going around the house on crutches. Despite having made the break from my troubled marriage, I still felt terribly depressed and anxious. It didn't help that I was in a custody battle with my soon-to-be ex-wife and spending half my monthly salary on alimony, child support, and lawyer bills. Every day was a struggle. I couldn't seem to find pleasure in anything.

Then, one morning at my new townhouse, I was standing by the stove making oatmeal for breakfast. Oatmeal has been a breakfast staple in my family ever since I was a kid. My mother used to make a huge pot of Quaker Oats every morning during the winter months. In addition to being inexpensive, oatmeal feeds a lot of people, tastes great, and is good for you. And so, when I had kids of my own, I kept up the tradition of making oatmeal in the mornings. Cut up some apples in it, add cinnamon and brown sugar and some walnuts, and you have the perfect breakfast, in my book.

So there I was, stirring a big pot of oatmeal while mulling on how bad I still felt despite working so hard at getting better. I had just tossed away yet another psychotropic prescription written by my script-pusher psychiatrist. Like all the other drugs she had given me, the med came with nasty side effects that only made me feel worse.

As I stirred the pot, smelling the warm aroma of apple and cinnamon and recalling homey memories of breakfasts in the kitchen of the old farmhouse, I became aware of a faint ray of pleasure opening up somewhere within my vast inner darkness. A few things struck me then: First, I was still able to feel pleasure, even the tiniest ray of it, when I had begun to fear the well of pleasure within me had dried up forever. Second, it was the smell of the oatmeal and the happy memories that came with it that was creating this inner pleasure response within me. Third, what I was feeling was a chemical reaction—likely a shot of dopamine—being released into my bloodstream.

I knew about the chemistry of depression, the effects that adrenaline and cortisol and other stress chemicals can have on your body. I knew the role that stress played in releasing those chemicals into the body. I knew that our thinking and perceptions had a lot to do with how our body reacted to stressors and other external stimuli.

I knew as well that this complicated process of external stimulus-perception-chemical response was exaggerated in me because of my inner sensitivity. I clearly had a biological tendency toward depression and anxiety that I was born with. But I also knew that I hadn't been born in this miserable state. Through the first twenty years or so of my life, and through most of my thirties as well, I was really a very happy person. My normal state of being was happiness and joy. It was only when I allowed myself to get wrapped around the axle of my inner conflicts that I got myself in trouble.

Which was where I was at now. Over the past four years, it struck me, I'd been hit with a perfect storm of life stressors: marital troubles, separation from my wife, moving out of my home, my skiing accident and surgery, financial worries. All these things would be stressful for anyone, but for me, they were tinder for a fire. My ruminating mind had fanned the flames with all its worrying and catastrophizing. As a result, my nervous system had been thrown into severe overload. My body, responding to the alarm signals my mind was sending, thought it was under attack and was pumping out stress signals like an intravenous line.

I had been in that state of emergency for so long that I had flipped the switch, so to speak, of my internal chemistry.

What this indicated to me, as I stood there by the stove stirring the pot of oatmeal, was that I had some control over my emotional states. I was not merely a helpless vial in some mad scientist's sick chemistry experiment. I was the chemist mixing that vial of chemicals. And if I was able to flip the switch of my internal chemistry into a state of imbalance by dwelling on the negative things happening in my life, then I should be able to flip it back into balance by focusing on positive things that would release the feel-good chemicals into my bloodstream.

The flicker of pleasure I felt with the oatmeal was proof that I could still generate those happiness chemicals. I just needed to do more of it. I needed to do it day after day after day: looking for things to be grateful for, giving thanks for them, and in the process releasing tiny shots of dopamine into my bloodstream until the good chemicals flooded out the bad ones, and my whole internal chemistry got back into balance.

It was an experiment. I didn't know if it would work. But it seemed logical, and what did I have to lose? Why rely on the mechanism of external pharmaceutical agents, with all their awful side effects, when I might be able to bring myself back from clinical depression on my own?

# The Gratitude Experiment: Looking for Blessings

So began the gratitude experiment. From the moment I woke up in the morning, I went about my day deliberately seeking things to be grateful for and offering thanks for them. They were everywhere, once I started looking for them:

The smell of the apple-cinnamon oatmeal wafting up from the pot.

The sweetness of softened apples in my mouth.

The lingering taste of cinnamon on my tongue.

The trail of warmth traveling down my throat into my belly.

With each little blessing that I experienced, I would add a silent prayer of gratitude:

*Praise you, Lord.*

*Praise you.*

Adding that prayer at the end was important for me. It wasn't just the gratitude expressed in those five words. It was the act of giving myself over to a higher power. For me, that higher power is Christian. But the higher power could also be Yahweh, Allah, the Buddha, the Universal Divine, or another creative, life-giving source of love and positivity. The act of giving oneself over to that higher power is essential to releasing the powers of gratitude, just as it is in the twelve-step program of Alcoholics Anonymous. Something about those simple words—*Praise you, Lord; praise you*—serves to disable the controlling levers of the ego-mind, releasing us into the abundant arms of the spirit.

And so, I went about my day, practicing the gratitude experiment. When my ego-mind protested—*This is stupid! This won't work!*—I would just acknowledge the negative thought, smile, and refocus my attention on acknowledging my blessings:

The heat of the fire on a cold winter's day.

The soothing patter of the rain on the roof.

The fact that I have a roof over my head.

The fact that I have a job to pay for that roof over my head.

The fact that a company has found my skills valuable enough to employ me and pay me a salary to take care of myself and my children.

*Praise you, Lord.*

*Praise you.*

It wasn't enough that I just thought about the blessing. I needed to *feel* it. I needed to feel that flicker of pleasure in my belly just as I had while smelling the oatmeal. To get that feeling in my belly, my gratitude had to be genuine. I had to be genuinely grateful for this blessing or else it wouldn't work. And so when I found something to be thankful for, I would pause, close my eyes, and really focus on and savor the blessing, while saying the magic words:

*Praise you, Lord.*

*Praise you.*

When I felt that spark of pleasure in my belly, I knew I was doing it right. Just like with the oatmeal, all the ingredients needed to be there for the recipe to work: the active search for the blessing; the acknowledgment that it was, in fact, a blessing; the engagement of my five senses in the blessing; the savoring of the blessing; the gratitude for the blessing; the happy spark of pleasure in my belly. That spark of pleasure was dopamine, being injected into my bloodstream not by an outside pharmaceutical agent, but by my own thoughts.

It became a practice. Mindful gratitude. And like with anything else, the more I practiced, the better I got at it. I was training my task-seeking mind to find reasons to be happy rather than reasons to be miserable.

The better I got at it, the better I felt. Day by day, week by week, the window of light within me grew as a percentage of the darkness—five percent, ten percent, twenty, thirty, forty—until, after a while, the light outshone the darkness.

As this happened, my moods stabilized. I became less depressed and anxious. My windows of peacefulness expanded day by day. Within six months, I was feeling normal again.

It had worked. I had flipped my inner chemistry back to its natural-born state. Now it was just a matter of keeping it going.

## Making Gratitude a Habit

More than ten years on from my chemistry experiment, I have kept it going.

I have had no more plunges into clinical depression. No more walks through darkness. No more weeks-long spells of anxiety where I want to crawl out of my own skin.

I take one little pill every day—ten milligrams of the antidepressant paroxetine, the minimum I can get in a prescription—which I continue to take because I've been on it for twenty years and it's so hard to get off the damn thing without a lot of side effects. Other than that, I rely on no other antidepressants or anti-anxiety medications.

My daily dose of medicine is gratitude. I keep my moods balanced and happy through a regular self-care regimen of sleep, exercise, nutrition, meditation, and appreciation.

I make it a point each day to actively look and giving thanks for the little things, like this slice of pizza. This pizza, bought for two dollars and fifty cents, is a mystic link to the spirit.

I take the last bite, bringing my awareness to the flavors: the sauce, the cheese, the spices, the crust. God, I love pizza.

*Praise you, Lord.*

*Praise you.*

Ten years ago, my days were so filled with darkness that I didn't think it was possible I would ever feel happy or peaceful again. Today, I am outside on a lovely October day enjoying a slice of pizza while soaking up the sun, the air, the smell of the fall leaves. Life is truly awesome.

Sure, I get down now and then, as everyone does. But it doesn't last long before I become conscious of what I'm doing inside me and I make a different choice. I have learned that every moment is a choice:

Do we want to step onto the path of negativity or the path of positivity?

The path of despair and hopelessness, or the path of joy and hopefulness?

The path of disillusionment or the path of appreciation?

Two forks diverge in a woods and which one we choose makes all the difference.

*Praise you, Lord.*

*Praise you!*

# 12

# The Other Side of Faith

*Hope is the thing with feathers*
*That perches in the soul*
*And sings the tune without the words*
*And never stops at all.*

—Emily Dickinson

The pizza slice has left a faint trace of grease on my fingers. What's pizza without a little grease?

    I lean down to wipe my fingers on the grass and walk on. I'm in a mostly residential neighborhood mixed with scattered commercial establishments. Sidewalks on my side of the road make for easier going than some of the earlier stretches that I've been walking over the past few hours. I pass a discount tire store, a credit union, and a self-storage facility for people who need room to keep all the stuff they don't use.

## Off the Straight and Narrow Path

Beyond the storage units, I pass a Roman Catholic elementary school and church. I have gone to a few services at this church in the past but I'm not a member. Officially, I am a registered member of another Catholic church in the area, although these days I am not a regular there or anywhere else. Despite the best efforts of the Sisters of Saint Joseph nuns during my twelve years of Catholic schooling, I have gradually drifted away from organized religion. It's not that I don't believe in God. I believe in God very strongly, just not the narrow and compartmentalized version of God I hear coming from so many churches I've attended over the years.

I could blame my falling away on the Church's sexual abuse and coverup scandal, which in truth has shocked me awake like a bucket of ice poured over my head. I could blame it on Sister Angela, the nun I had in elementary school who used to drag bad boys out of class to knock their heads on the outside classroom wall, and who once struck me with a ruler on the knuckles for talking in class when I had just been sitting there being good.

I could blame it on the devil himself, but I don't believe in the devil, at least not the way I learned in religion class.

In truth, it was life itself, rather than the deeds of fallible men and women, that led me away from the Church, and the Church away from me. It was life that took me off the straight and narrow path of catechism texts into a messy, tangled swamp where the stuff I learned in Catholic school either wasn't relevant or served only to remind me what a sinful, broken person I was.

Generally speaking, I find there are two camps of people who went through the full complement of twelve years of Catholic education: There are those enviable souls who absorbed all those teachings and continue to faithfully attend Sunday services and recite the Profession of Faith, even if they don't necessarily believe or practice everything they're saying. And then there are the lapsed souls like me who have shed our Catholic uniforms because they don't fit us any longer. We are divorced or separated. We are gay, bisexual, or don't know what our sexual orientation is. We question the fundamental tenets of the Church, such as the infallibility of the Pope, the celibacy of the priesthood, or the fact that only men can become rule-making priests and elders of the church. We have drunk from the troughs of Buddhism and other Eastern enlightenment practices that aren't officially accepted by the Church and yet have brought peace to our souls, including release from the heavy guilt we feel for not having lived up to the standards of what it means to be an acceptable child of God.

Yes, we get official pronouncements from the Church that we misfits are still welcome to the communion table. That we are God's people like everyone else. That we can come to the altar, sins and warts and all. But there are exclusions. A lot of them. If we're divorced, we must not have remarried outside the Church. If we are gay or lesbian or transsexual, we must not be practicing our sexual preferences. If we are doing yoga, we must be doing it for the physical benefits and not as part of a deeper spiritual practice that does not conform to official Church doctrine.

And so we skulk away like scolded lepers to find a more inclusive community that will accept us as we are. I often discuss this with my girlfriend, who is also Catholic and divorced and, by the way, a yoga teacher. We love many things about the religion we grew up with, most particularly the sacraments and the gorgeous communion service. But why must we be or think a certain way in order to lay out our tongues for the host? Must spirit be defined in a narrow, rigid way in order to be experienced? Who thought of all these rules, and what do they have to do with Christ's teachings of love, kindness, acceptance, and forgiveness?

## The Muddy Waters of Institutional Doctrine

I struggle with churches for the same reason that I struggle with big corporations. Both are institutions, only of different stripes. Both are leviathans with their own interests and self-preservation in mind, and experience has taught me that when self-interested institutions get involved in anything—particularly something as pure and beautiful as spirituality—the waters are going to get muddy very quickly.

The waters get muddy when institutions begin to codify abstractions into official doctrine and policies that seek to judge, limit, or redirect the individual experience and expression of the spirit. At that point, policy begins to trump experience, doctrine gets confused with intention, and politics crowd out beauty as sure as thistles choke flowers in a garden.

Doctrine and policies have an important role to play in pointing us to the truth, but they are not the truth itself. The truth can only truly be known when it is experienced, and that happens at an individual level. There is the stuff of the head and then there is the stuff of the spirit, and the two are not the same. The map is not the territory. Doctrines are not real. Standards are not real. Precepts are not real. They are abstractions—stuff of the head, not the heart. What is real is the way the spirit manifests and expresses itself within individual people, and that experience is as unique as snowflakes. No preacher or catechism textbook can tell someone how this should happen.

Don't get me wrong: There is much that is good about religion and churches, and I am poorer in many ways for not being closely associated with one. One day soon, I hope to part of one again.

But for now, where I am in my journey, a church doesn't work for me. When it comes to practicing my faith, I need a wide margin. I seek to experience life as directly as possible, without the distorted filters of doctrine and dogma. I try, best as I am able, to live the example of Jesus by practicing kindness and non-judgmental acceptance of people and of life itself. I do that not just because it's the right thing to do, but because it makes me feel good, and when I feel good, I know I am in the spirit and not in my head.

## Self-Inflicted Wounds

All this gets me thinking about the nature of faith and the role faith has played in carrying me through the many ups and downs of my life.

Every family seems to have one person who draws drama like iron filings to a magnet, and in my family, that person is me. I've lost track of all the surgeries and medical procedures I've had, how many trips to hospital emergency rooms, how many dark nights of the soul. My life's drama started early and continued steady as a soap opera:

- At the age of six, during a big family party at our little farm to celebrate my father's graduation from night school, I fell while playing badminton in the back field. When I stood up, my arm was bent in the wrong direction, and I ran screaming past startled aunts and uncles and cousins to the house, where I was swept into the car and driven to the emergency room to spend the night in the hospital while everyone else was partying.
- The following year, during another family party at our house, I was playing Ghost in the Graveyard with my siblings and cousins when I tripped and fell, landing face down on the concrete and breaking my front

tooth in half—necessitating an emergency trip to the dentist for a cap that remains to this day.

- At the age of nineteen while working a summer construction job—not, in retrospect, a wise occupation for a daydreamer like me—I nearly cut my right hand off with a circular saw while laying down a new roof. The saw cut through five tendons, bone, and an artery, producing a gusher of blood and necessitating a wild ambulance ride to Philadelphia for emergency surgery followed by six months of hand therapy. Thanks to the work of those amazing doctors and therapists at the Jefferson University Hand Center, I was able in time to gain most of the functionality of my right hand—a truly fortuitous and blessed outcome given the fact that I went on to make my living typing on keyboards.
- At thirty-two, I tore cartilage in my knee while playing basketball and underwent arthroscopic surgery.
- At thirty-eight, I underwent hernia surgery to repair the damage from lifting a railroad tie by myself while working in the backyard.
- Six years later came the skiing accident while I was in the middle of divorce proceedings with my wife. There I was, coming around a bend, the picture of suave and grace, when I lost control and slid backward into a fence. My head hit hard on the steel post (stupidly, I wasn't wearing a helmet) and I blacked out for a few seconds. When I came to, I was on the ground with my left leg turned grotesquely beneath me. The ski patrol took me down the slope on a sled

and then it was off to surgery to have Humpty Dumpty put back together again.

- Then, six years after that, I went in for the routine colonoscopy and began my journey through cancer. Fortunately, the doctors found the tumor early enough to do something about it, and so it was back to the operating table for surgery to take out a foot of my colon followed by six months of chemotherapy, infusion balls, nausea, neuropathy, mouth sores, and otherwise grand fun.

This doesn't count my two episodes of clinical depression, the twelve rounds of ECT, and all the years of my life I lost wrestling with the black beast.

Do I believe that I'm cursed? That I have bad luck?

Of course not. This is life. Things happen, and I see now, in retrospect, that most of the things that have happened to me were self-inflicted. Not consciously, of course. It's not that I wanted to create pain for myself. It's just that I lacked awareness of the complex set of levers that operated my inner manifesting machine. Awareness is everything when it comes to living a contented, peaceful life, and for the first forty-some years of my life, my inner manifesting machine was working on autopilot. It was driving me, rather than the other way around.

But I'm still here, and there's a reason for that, too. I am alive because, throughout all my many years of mostly self-inflicted darkness and suffering, my desire to live was stronger than the demons within that sought my destruction.

I am alive, you are alive, we are all alive at this moment because we choose to be. To be or not to be—that is the question we get to answer for ourselves every moment of every day of our lives. Within our psyches is an inner scale against which we weigh those two fundamental options. On the "To Be" side of the scale are all the reasons why we choose to live: for the joys of family and relationships; for the pleasures of food, sex, adventures, travel; for the responsibility we feel toward our children, communities, and the world in general; for the fulfillment we get from work and making use of our talents and gifts for some higher purpose.

On the "Not to Be" side are reasons why we may not want to live: illness, disease, chronic pain and suffering, trauma, loneliness, financial issues. All of these can fuel feelings of deep hopelessness and desperation.

For most of us, most of the time, there's a lot more on the "To Be" side than on the "Not to Be" side, and the choice to continue living is as easy and natural as breathing. We don't need to consciously think about it. We just go on breathing, though the choice to stop doing so is always there.

But, as is evident from the rising suicide rates in our country, there are a lot of suffering people out there, people whose scales have tipped more toward the "Not to Be" side of the scale. The simple joys and pleasures of life are unavailable to them, or appear to be. They may have felt those joys and pleasures in the past—almost certainly, they have. But now, for whatever reason, those joys and pleasures have dried up. Their days are dark and heavy and colorless.

For these suffering souls, the choice of whether to be or not to be shifts from unconscious to conscious mode. Does the "Not to Be" side of their scale outweigh their "To Be" side? Which is stronger: their wanting to live or their wanting to be free of the pain of being alive?

## Faith: The Substance of Things Hoped for

I have faced that choice in a very real way within my own life. When I was going through my second clinical depression during my forties as my marriage was falling apart, I was haunted by thoughts of driving my car to a nearby quarry and plunging to the rocks below. The vision of that quarry was so clear, so vivid, so tantalizing. It was the only way my exhausted ego could think of to end the unremitting pain I was living in.

Every day back then, death spoke to me, whispering in my ear in dulcet tones, offering a way out of my inner hell: Just head over to the quarry and drive my car over the cliff. Ten seconds of terror and then the pain would be over.

Why didn't I listen to that dark voice? Why did I continue on? Why does anyone continue on in the face of suffering?

We go on because we have faith that we are more than our present circumstances. We go on because we believe those circumstances won't last, that things will get better, perhaps in spite of all evidence otherwise. Isn't that what faith is all about? Churches can put a lot of rules and doctrine around it, but in the end, faith is a simple thing. The apostle Paul said it best in that wonderful line from his letter to the Hebrews (11:1, KJV): "Now faith is the substance of things hoped for, the evidence of things not seen."

I've always loved that quote, the way the apostle uses scientific words to describe the power of faith. Faith is not an ineffable thing, he's saying. It is substance. It is the tangible evidence of something very real and powerful, if only we believe that to be so.

As I walk now on this beautiful October afternoon, I find myself giving quiet thanks to my mother who, more than any sermon or catechism text, taught me the true power of faith in working miracles in my life. When my world came crashing down during my first clinical depression, my mother would talk to me for countless hours over the phone as I fought to keep my composure at the little newspaper office where I worked at the time. I was only a kid then, all of twenty-one years old. I didn't know what truck had run over me. I was convinced that my life was over, that I would never feel normal and happy again.

My mother, a woman of deep Christian belief, would calmly speak to me of her own past sufferings with depression and anxiety, how her faith got her through, how God never gives you more than you can handle, how tough times never last but tough people do. Her words were so firm, so certain. There was not a shadow of a doubt in them.

"When you get to the other side of this," she told me, "you're going to feel so good about yourself, Jim."

Twenty years later, when my marriage was failing and I fell back deep into the pit of depression, my mother was there for me once again. We would sit on the front porch of the old farmhouse gliding back and forth on the creaky old rocking chairs, talking through the seemingly insolvable dilemma of my situation.

"Can't resolve it?" she would ask me as I told her about my conflicted feelings about the marriage.

I shook my head. "I work so hard at it, Mom. I just can't figure out what to do."

"Maybe you're trying too hard," she said.

"What do you mean?"

"You're not going to figure this out on your own. Give it over to God."

She'd been saying this for years to us. Whenever one of her kids was struggling with something that felt too big to solve, she'd tell us to "give it over." Hand the problem over to God. Let Him figure it out.

But what did that mean? What was I supposed to do exactly? My whole life, I'd been trained to do things. That's the way you solve problems. You analyze the issue, figure out the root cause, create a plan, gather the tools you need, and execute. It was the blueprint I'd followed for every success and achievement in my life, whether in school or in my career. And now I was supposed to throw up my hands and sit there? It made no sense.

"Are you praying?" she asked me.

"I pray every day. Nothing comes back to me."

She gave a knowing nod. "Well, keep praying," she said.

We would sit out on that porch for hours. I remember how dark my mind was then. Nothing gave me pleasure. Nothing was able to break through the blackness of my days. I felt lost on a black, storm-swept sea as the waves tossed me about like a toy boat. How I must have wearied her, going over the same old ground, the same hopeless feelings, the same unresolvable issues.

But if she felt frustrated, my mother never showed it. Most days, she would have her rosary with her, and she would just sit there on the chair, gently rocking back and forth as her arthritic hands fingered the rosewood beads. Birds chirped, cars swooshed by on the road, neighbors would walk past on the pavement across the street and give a wave. We rocked and rocked and rocked, the wood runners of our chairs crunching on dried-up seed pods blown onto the porch from the big catalpa tree that overhung the house, while I talked and my mother listened.

"You need to get to the other side of this, Jim," she would say, again and again. "When you get to the other side, things will look different."

She was right. It took a long time, but I did get to the other side, and it did look different. Faith paid off. If I had given up to the voice of desperation that bid me to plunge my car into the quarry, how much life and joy I would have missed.

## Getting to the Other Side

The other side.

Those three words, simple as they are, have always been the bedrock of my mother's faith. I learned through her that trouble is a dark tunnel, but it's a tunnel that does not go on forever. On the other side is light and joy, and we need only keep walking, keep believing, keep looking for the good, and we will get to the other side.

Such is the mystery of faith of which the apostle Paul speaks: to believe in something even though there is no tangible evidence of it in the present moment. Thinking won't get you there. Reasoning won't get you there. Drowning in your sorrows won't get you there. Only faith. Only believing.

This is the kind of faith that I practice. My faith is fundamentally pragmatic. Life is hard, or it can be, and I believe faith should provide comfort in our journey, not make life even harder by making us feel guilty or bad about ourselves. When I hit rough patches, I seek comfort in my belief in an all-loving, all-accepting, all-embracing spirit that I can tap into at any point by expressing gratitude for the simple joys and pleasures of being alive.

As for heaven—yes, I believe in heaven, but not as a place where you go because a deity has judged you worthy of being there, but rather as a dwelling place for my spirit when it has shrugged off the used-up coil of my body. I hold this belief in heaven because it gives me hope and comfort that there is even more wonder and joy coming after this life is over. Whether my belief in an afterlife turns out to be true or not, I get the benefits of feeling better today for holding that belief. So why not do it? What's the downside?

And if that doesn't accord with your vision of God or heaven or what it means to be saved, then I say: Go live your book and I will live mine, and let us be at peace with one another, and the world will be a better place because of it.

# 13

# Resilience

*What lies behind us and what lies before us are tiny matters compared to what lies within us.*

—Ralph Waldo Emerson

I'm well beyond the church now, my wayward train of thought having carried me another mile or so up the road on my solitary walk home.

Around a corner and down a hill, I come to a self-service car wash that has been out of service for a number of years after a fire. As I walk past, I note graffiti on a wall and burned-out vacuums that look like something out of a dystopian movie. I wonder what the story is behind the car wash, whether maybe the owner doesn't have insurance and can't afford to rebuild. Things can stay in stasis for a while after disaster strikes. Sometimes a disaster can be the final blow in a long series of hard knocks that leaves us flattened on the side of the road.

I can't allow that to happen to me. Got to keep walking, keep moving forward.

## Back in the Country

Beyond the deserted car wash, I pass over a bridge and, after ten miles or so of highway walking, I leave Route 202 and turn left onto Main Street. I am in Chalfont, a quaint little village of multicolored Victorian cottages in Bucks County, Pennsylvania. Like so many of the Main Streets that run through small American towns, there's not much to this street. I pass a coffee shop. A hair salon. An insurance agency. Farther up, I pass the municipal building and fire station.

And that's pretty much it. In five minutes, I'm out of town and back among residential homes again. Main Street quietly turns into Route 152, aka Limekiln Pike, so named for the loads of lime that were transported a century ago along this route from kilns to farms for sweetening fields and making ripe mixes of mortar.

I am back in the country, on the final stretch of my journey home. Whenever I would get to this point on my commute home from the office, I would allow myself a sigh of relief, once I was finally beyond the cities and towns, the traffic and congested intersections. Only a couple of traffic lights remain between me and home, and I can easily avoid them by taking back roads. No more stop lights, no stores, no shopping centers. Only woods and fields and the macadam roads that run through them. The driving is easy.

Walking here, however, is not so easy. The rural road is narrow and winding, and all the twists and turns make it hard for a walker like me to see approaching cars. Some stretches have no walkable shoulders at all and I need to tread on people's lawns.

As I cross the front yard of a rundown little cottage house nearly hidden among overgrown bushes, I'm startled by sight of a gray-haired woman sitting out on the front porch in a rocking chair. She is old and slouch-shouldered, her gnarly hands digging into the arms of the chair as if she's about to take a dip on a roller coaster. Her eyes follow me like a cat as she rocks back and forth.

"How about this day!" I call out cheerily. "Gorgeous!"

The old woman doesn't reply and just watches me suspiciously with her narrow cat eyes. She's probably not used to seeing people out walking on this back country road and thinks I'm either going to rob her or try to sell her something. You can't blame her. There are a lot of nuts out there. I give a little wave and continue on my way.

A soft breeze wafts over my face, smelling of autumn leaves. It really is a fantastic day, what with the crisp fall air and the sun shining overhead and the crimson maples accented against a sky as blue as a robin's egg. With every step I take, with every mile I put behind me, I feel a little better, a little clearer, though I still have no idea what I'm going to do when I lose my job. This walk itself is somehow giving me strength.

Isn't that how life works? What doesn't kill you makes you stronger, as long as you learn from your mistakes and don't give up. Keep walking, keep believing, and the road will take you through the tunnel to a better place. Each experience of getting through a challenge leaves us stronger and better equipped for the next tunnel coming down the pike.

Such is the power of experience. We labor on because this is not the first rough patch we've faced on our life's walk. We've been in tough places before and they didn't last. Better times returned, the sun came out again, we felt the old simple joys, and we have faith that we'll do so again.

The journey gives us strength.

## Lessons in Resilience from a Crabapple Tree

As soon as I have a chance, I turn right off Limekiln Pike onto a less-traveled back road where there is more shoulder room to walk.

The road takes me up a long, steep slope. Up I go, feeling the sweet burn in my calves. The breeze is in my face, cool as a fan, and I barely break a sweat as I walk. Halfway up the hill, I stop to catch my breath. The tree line to the right of me is thick and tangled and has been hacked away over the years by farmers and township road crews. I take note of a crabapple tree growing at the base of a rusted old steel pasture fence. The tree has twisted around the fence, incorporating the steel into its tangled trunk like a surgically repaired leg. Despite the injury, the tree has managed to grow fifteen feet high and is loaded with red-cheeked golden crabapples ripe for the picking.

I marvel at the tree's resilience. Resilience is the necessary complement of faith. Without it, faith has no mechanism, no forward movement. Resilience is the mental toughness and elasticity that allows us to take a blow, get back up, and keep going. The fire that put that car wash out of commission a couple of miles back may have dealt a fatal blow for the business. But for this crabapple tree, the steel fence hammered into its roots was just an obstacle to grow around.

I continue on up the hill, thinking about the steel plate in my leg from the surgery on my broken tibia after the ill-fated skiing trip. The surgeon who did the operation told me afterward that my leg, when fully healed, would be even stronger than it was before the accident. And now here I am, ten years later, walking more than twenty miles on that leg and it doesn't hurt at all. Bone and steel are fused together in blended strength, like the fence and the crabapple tree back there.

I never fail to be amazed by the resilience of the human spirit in the face of adversity. There are stories of that resilience everywhere. For me, one of the most inspiring is the story of the Austrian neurologist and Holocaust survivor Viktor Frankl, who wrote the classic book *Man's Search for Meaning* about his experiences in the Nazi concentration camps. Frankl lost his parents, his wife, his brother, many friends—essentially, everyone who was important to him—at Auschwitz and other camps. What kept him going?

According to Frankl in the book, it was his ability to choose his own attitude even in the midst of unspeakable atrocities and suffering. His German captors could take away everything else—his freedom, his clothes, his food, his family, even his life—but they could not take away his spiritual freedom to think his own independent thoughts and find hope and meaning in the darkness of circumstances.

We live in an age of hero worship, when Hollywood actors, music stars, beautiful models, and professional athletes are frequently held up to us as worthy of our attention and emulation. But to me, it's people like Frankl—everyday people who find themselves in tough circumstances and don't give up—who are the true heroes who light my way.

## Faith of My Father

I think of my great-great-grandfather James Delano Kerr, after whom I'm named. James Delano emigrated from Scotland in the late 1800s in search of better opportunities in America. His ship was supposed to land in Baltimore, but a port strike diverted him to Philadelphia. He knew no one in his new country and had nothing but a suitcase and the clothes on his back. But through his own persistence and ingenuity, he founded his own textile dyeworks company and was so successful that he was able to retire in his fifties.

I think as well of the example left behind by my father, who recently passed at the age of eighty-seven. My dad never attained fame or worldly status. He didn't make a lot of money and never attained a big, fancy title at the companies where he worked. But for me and my siblings, he provided an example of resilience and perseverance that lives on within us like rings in a tree trunk.

Like many people who grew up during the Depression, my father learned the lessons of resilience the hard way on the dairy farm where he grew up. His father, my grandfather, ran the family's textile dyeworks business in northeast Philadelphia. The dairy farm was a side business for the family, and the day-to-day management and duties of the farm fell to my father and his older brother. My dad would tell us stories of having to wake up at four-thirty on cold winter mornings to milk the cows before heading off to school. This was before the advent of indoor plumbing and other modern conveniences. When you needed to use the bathroom, you took a stroll outside to the outhouse to sit on a cold slab of wood above a hole in the ground.

The dyeworks was struggling and the family didn't have much money. In addition to his chores, my father contributed to the family finances by trapping muskrats for their pelts and raising and butchering domestic ducks for sale. It was a hard life, one that he knew he didn't want to continue when he was older, and so when it came time to choose a career, he decided to go to college to become an electrical engineer.

Halfway through his studies at Penn State, however, the dyeworks failed and my father came home to the news that his parents couldn't afford to continue his education. Undaunted, he got a job as an engineer at a local electronics plant and went to night school at Drexel to finish his degree. About this time, he married my mother and the kids started coming: five of us in the next eight years. He was now getting up at four-thirty in the morning, not to milk cows, but to study for school before going to work at the plant. After ten years of night school, he completed his studies and earned his degree in electrical engineering. In the meantime, he was being steadily promoted at the plant and eventually rose to the position of quality-control manager, with a team of people reporting to him.

Those were good years for our family. My father was making good money and was even given a company car. He and my mother were able to buy our six-acre farm in the countryside. But then, in 1971, the plant where he'd worked for eighteen years unexpectedly shut down and he lost his job. The plant was a division of Ford Motor Company, which at the time was pursuing an ill-fated strategy to diversify into consumer electronics. This was during the advent of integrated circuits that spawned companies like Intel. Ford, much like my own employer, hadn't anticipated the industry shift and got left in the dust. Thousands of people were let go from their jobs as the epicenter of the electronics universe shifted from the East Coast to Silicon Valley.

For my father, the loss of his long-held corporate job was more than a financial shock. It represented to him a betrayal of an unspoken oath between him and his employer, an oath that he took nearly as seriously as his marriage vows. He had gotten the job right out of school, and like many people in that day, he had expected to spend the rest of his career there. There was, in his mind, an implicit bargain that you made when you signed up to work for a big company: You gave the firm your full energies and talents, and it, in turn, gave you its loyalty.

For the first eighteen years, that bargain had played out as my father expected. Now, it was all gone. To add salt to the wound, the firm had let him go just a year and a half before he would have vested for a pension. Around the house and at the dinner table, he raged like King Lear at the company that had tossed him aside.

"Sons of bitches!"

"Eighteen years I gave to that company and they throw me away right before my pension vests!"

I didn't know what a pension was or why it was important. All I knew was that after all the happy years on our little farm, things were suddenly very tense and dark in our household. My youngest sister had just been born, which meant another mouth to feed. My father went looking for a position at another company, but the economy was in the tank and good jobs were hard to find. For a period of time, we didn't have medical insurance—a scary proposition for a single-income household with six kids, including one as injury-prone as I was.

With my inner sensitivity, I could feel the toll these trials were having on my mother. I was used to seeing her happy smile as she went about the house, hearing her humming upbeat tunes while she readied our breakfasts in the morning before school. Now, her cheery disposition wilted like a rose in a dried-up vase. Her face was drawn and she rarely smiled. I could sense her sadness, her worry. She would sometimes slip out of the room and go lie down upstairs in her room. When she came down, her eyes were swollen. Other times, I would see her out on the front porch sitting on the rocking chair, the beads of her rosary wrapped around her hands.

I desperately wanted my father to stop his raging. I wanted him to pray like my mother did. I wanted him to go to church with us on Sunday mornings and take the communion host on his tongue. But unlike my mother, my dad took no stock in religion. The only times in his life when he ever set foot in a church were for weddings, baptisms, or funerals. His faith was of a different kind. He believed in a faith that comes from facing adversity with bull-headed determination and perseverance, and we saw that brand of faith play out in very real ways following his dismissal from the electronics plant.

## Battle Cry: Heroes in the Strife

As the weeks went by, his words, though still angry, also grew firm and steady. A resolve formed within him. "Never give up," he would say to us through clenched teeth, in his overly dramatic way of talking. "When the forces of evil are arrayed against you, never, ever, ever give up. Be a hero in the strife."

The "never give up" stuff came from Winston Churchill when he rallied his besieged country to resist Hitler and the Nazis during World War II. The "hero in the strife" stuff came from his beloved Longfellow poem, which we heard a lot of during those uncertain months after he lost his job:

Be not like dumb, driven cattle!
Be a hero in the strife!

Those lines were my father's battle cry. As bitter as it was to swallow what had happened to him, he didn't do what many men do and head to the local bar to drink away his sorrows. That was herd behavior. He had responsibilities to live up to and he was determined to live up to them.

And so, a hero in the strife, my father set out to make ends meet for his family as he looked for another job. He studied for his real-estate license and began selling and renting houses through a local realtor. Sometimes those settlement and rental checks were all we had to go on to buy groceries for the month.

He also fell back on his love of the land to make a living. With the help of an old 8N Ford tractor and a host of farm implements bought secondhand, he plowed a section of the side hay field to start his vegetable garden. He started with the basics—sweet corn, tomatoes, beans, beets, carrots—adding new varieties of vegetables every year until eventually, the garden took up the entire two-acre side lot of our little farm.

That garden became our family's personal food source. What didn't go to the dinner table, my mother froze and jarred for dinners through the winter months. He and my mother also set up a roadside stand to sell farm-fresh vegetables. The sweet corn was the biggest hit. Back then, you could sell a dozen ears for two bucks—not a lot of money for all the work that went into growing the corn, but every dollar counted in our household. The dollars we got from the roadside stand went into a jar that my mother kept on a cabinet shelf in the kitchen. I remember her bringing down that jar on school mornings to hand us our lunch money for the day.

## The Scars That Make Us Stronger

With the help of the vegetable garden and a lot of novenas said by my mother, things would eventually settle down for our family.

My father found another job in New Jersey that required a ninety-minute drive each way to and from the office. The smile returned to my mother's face. I would hear her humming again at the breakfast table in the morning.

Life went on at our little farm. But things were not the same as before. Things never fully go back to the way they were before after we experience a major adversity. That's what I've found, at least. Circumstances are different, and we are different, too. We have the scars, and the scars make us stronger.

My father only lasted a year at the job in New Jersey before he got tired of the commute and found another position closer to home. That new company, however, was soon acquired, and he was again out of work for a while. In all, he persevered through five different companies until he finally found work at a local electronics plant where he would spend the last fifteen years of his career. In each of those jobs, he never exceeded the salary he'd been making when Ford let him go.

This fact ate at him for the rest of his life. He'd learned his lesson and would never put all of himself into a company again. Every job after that first one at the electronics plant was just a way to make money, and nothing more.

"Never trust a company, kids," he would warn us. "Give them your life and they throw you away. The only people you can trust in this world are your family. Always remember that."

The irony of this hits me as I come to the top of the hill I'm walking. I ended up working even longer at one company than my father did. How is that possible? Did I not listen to his advice?

Actually, I did listen. I listened very closely to every word my dad said while I was growing up. I absorbed his distrust of institutions the way a stalk of corn absorbs nutrients from the soil where it's planted.

But being the sensitive soul I am, I also absorbed the heavy uncertainty that hung in the air during those years when our family was living paycheck to paycheck, agonizing over which bills to pay first and where to find the money for Catholic school, for college, for the oil company to come and fill our tank to provide heat for the winter ahead. Living for so many years amid that insecurity has made me cautious. It made me want my own kids never to have to feel that kind of financial insecurity. It has led me to place a premium on stability over risk-taking.

That's why now, after nearly twenty-eight years at the company, I find myself walking in my father's shoes. What he went through, I am now going through. The difference is that my dad was thirty-nine when he lost his first job. I am about to turn fifty-six, and I'm at an entirely different point in my career.

How will I respond to this adversity in my life? What example will I leave my children?

Will I overcome or be overcome?

# 14

# In the Company of Trees

*In solitude the mind gains strength and learns to lean on itself.*

—Laurence Sterne

I labor onward to the top of the hill, where I am rewarded with a gorgeous view of a wooded valley stretching out below me. The sun, beginning to descend toward the horizon to the west, casts a golden glow across the landscape, revealing a dream coat of red, orange, and bronze. In the distance,

I see the shimmering waters of Lake Galena, where I often go walking and kayaking.

The view of the resplendent fall foliage cheers me in a way that all my pep talks over the past few hours could not. Some people see fall as a reason to get down because it means winter and cold weather are right around the corner. Not me. I enjoy all the seasons and look forward to each of them for what they have to offer. I love the simplicity of winter, the way everything is stripped back to its essence. I can put aside the lawn mowing, weeding, garden work, and all the other outdoor chores and turn to things I didn't have time to do during the busy summer months. Like reading.

## Nature: The Ultimate Optimist

I look forward to winter, too, for anticipation of what follows it: the renewal and rejuvenation of spring. Nature is the ultimate optimist. Put her through the harshest winter and she'll come back greener than ever in the spring. Chop her down and she'll send out new shoots in unexpected places. Place an obstacle in her path and she'll grow around it, like that crabapple tree back there. Burn her down and she'll rise like the phoenix, finding within the scorched earth the nutrients she needs to produce ever-greater diversity.

I just love that. I love not just the seasonal rejuvenation but the rebirth that happens in nature every day. It's why I enjoy the mornings so much. Yesterday may have been an awful day, the worst day of your life, but today is a new day filled with fresh possibility, if only you look for it. Another quote from Thoreau's *Walden* comes to me:

> *To him whose vigorous and elastic thought keeps pace with the sun, the day is a perpetual morning.*

We human beings tend to think of ourselves as somehow separate from nature, but we're not. We are born of the sun, so why can't we keep our thinking aligned with the sun? Imagine that: each day rising onto new continents, new vistas, new days, new moments; each day leaving behind the night and all its dark imaginings and looking ahead to new adventures and possibilities.

Why is it so hard for us to think like that? Why do we allow ourselves to be defeated so easily when the force that created us is never defeated? The alternative is much better. Let us strap ourselves on the back of the sun and allow it to take us to new lands each and every day, firm in the knowledge that the storm will pass, the clouds will break, the darkness will fade, the fire will be extinguished, and we will rise from the ashes, stronger than ever.

How much better we'll feel if we think that way! We don't need to turn away from the tough stuff of life, but we can approach it with faith, optimism, and resilience. They're all entwined, and we can see their miraculous workings every day in the rejuvenating cycles of nature.

Even death. Why do we need to view death as an end? Why not view it as nature views it: as an opportunity for renewal and new life? We aren't just bodies, after all. We are spirits, part of the greater spirit that joins all things.

Does a river fear the ceasing of its flow? Does the Earth fear no longer spinning?

This, I think, is the way I need to view my current situation. Approach it like that crabapple tree did: A stake has been driven into my path, but I've had lots of obstacles in my way before and I haven't let them stop me.

I am resilient.

I am optimistic.

I've been down before and will rise again, in a way that perhaps I'm not expecting.

Let me ride the sun and see where it takes me.

## Forests: Portals into the Spirit

The road cuts through a thick forest, blocking off my view of the valley. I'm surrounded by huge oaks and hickory trees. Dropped acorns and hickory nuts crunch beneath my shoes. The fading sunlight fans down through the canopy of leaves overhead, warming my face.

I take a breath of the crisp fall air, drawing it deep into my lungs. My senses stir. I am alone, yet not alone. I am one, yet all. I am infinitesimal, yet infinite.

Ah, how I love being in the woods! Especially woods made up of old-growth hardwood trees, like you often find here in Pennsylvania. The deeper the woods and the older the trees, the better. Give me a forest free of roads and paths and other humanmade enhancements, free of noise from highways and lawnmowers and buzzing utility lines, free of the stink of car exhaust and factories and meat-rendering plants. When

I go into the woods, I want to hear only the sound of the wind and smell only the scent of pine needles and damp soil. There are still woods where I can find such peace, and those are the places I seek out whenever I have the time and the opportunity—places like the Endless Mountains of northeastern Pennsylvania, the New York Catskills, the Rocky Mountains of Colorado, and other national parks.

There is something profoundly spiritual about being in a forest. To stand among majestic oaks and elms arching a hundred feet over your head, gazing up at the sunlight filtering down through the canopy of leaves, stirs the deepest regions of the soul as much as stepping into the magnificent cathedrals of Florence and Milan. Forests are portals into the spirit. Enter the community of trees and feel at home there. See the beauty of God's handiwork. Hear the spirit speaking in tongues through the stirring of the leaves. Know you will not be judged there or denied admission to the table. All are welcome, regardless of race, gender, age, sexual preference, or political views.

Churches can be such a sanctuary, too, and the best ones are. But so many of today's churches have allowed the judgment and politics of the outside world to seep inside their walls and drown out whatever spirit dwells there. To me, this is where religion takes leave of spirituality, where religion fails in its mission. Give me the choice between spending time in a church or the deep woods and I will choose the woods. Trees don't have rules or exclusions. Trees don't judge, dissemble, or take political stands. Trees don't say one thing and do another. Trees don't prey on the innocent and protect the guilty.

So I seek the woods. Over the course of my life, I suspect that I have spent nearly as much time in the company of trees as in the company of people. Trees are good company. They are also good teachers. I have learned a lot from them about the virtues of patience, resilience, equanimity, and steadfastness in the face of adversity. The wisdom of trees is ancient and timeless, and they impart their wisdom without need of words, flashy images, or autoplay video ads. I learn more every time I'm in their company.

## An Early Hunting Lesson from My Father

I owe my love of the outdoors to my father, who was steeped in it from the time he was little. Even his middle name, Forrest, which he generally went by with his family and acquaintances, was carved from the woods.

My dad loved to hunt, fish, camp, boat, garden, and just about anything else that involved being outside, and he shared that love with his children. Before my brothers and I were even old enough to hunt, we would walk by his side as he carried his double-barrel shotgun through the sounding woods on cool fall mornings. Though we were out in search of squirrels, rabbits, and pheasants, much of the time instead my father was imparting instruction. How to walk quietly through the woods. How to play the wind to your advantage while stalking deer. How to drive a stubbled cornfield for ring-neck pheasants.

Safety was always at the center of these lessons. I remember the first time he allowed me to shoot a gun. I was eleven years old, and my father had taken me out into the back field behind the house and set up a tin can in an apple tree twenty-five yards away. Then he strode back to me and handed the shotgun to me. It was a simple, single-shot gun designed for junior hunters. My older brother had used the shotgun when he began hunting but had since moved onto a pump shotgun, so now the gun was mine to use.

It was a crisp Saturday morning in October, much like this day, except colder. The apple tree had lost its leaves and held the tin can in a clutch of craggy fingers. I was eager to blast that can out of the tree, but my father had the shotgun shells in his pocket and didn't look ready to hand one to me.

"I want you to hold the gun for a couple minutes," he said. "Get a sense how it feels."

So I stood there in the deepening morning, feeling the weight of the gun in my hands. It felt like the Daisy BB rifle that I shot birds with, except longer and heavier. The stock was made of real wood, not plastic, and the barrel was steel: long and sleek with a bead at the end for aiming. To load the gun, you flipped a lever on the receiver and the chamber broke open. My father had me do that, but still, he didn't give me a shotgun shell.

"That gun could kill someone," he said sternly, nodding at it in my hands.

"I know," I said with all the cockiness of an eleven-year-old.

"No, you don't know. It only takes one mistake and someone's dead. Or you're dead. Understand?"

"Yes."

"Don't ever point the gun at anyone," he said firmly. "If you're not shooting, you keep the barrel pointed up in the air or at the ground. And never load it in the house."

I knew all this already from the Pennsylvania Hunter Safety course that I'd taken and passed, but I nodded dutifully.

"The minute I ever see you horsing around with a gun, it gets taken away."

"I'm never going to do that."

"Okay, here," he said, handing me the twenty-gauge shell.

He eyed me closely as I dropped the shell into the chamber and closed it.

"Now, pull back the hammer," he instructed. "Good. Keep your finger away from the trigger until you're ready to fire. Now, get yourself set. Make sure the butt is tight up against your shoulder. There. Now, close your left eye and aim down the barrel. That's it. Now, gently squeeze . . ."

The gun went off. The tin can fell out of the tree. I smelled gunpowder in the air.

My father was beaming. "You did it!"

The gun's kick was harder than I had expected. My shoulder hurt, but I didn't care. I had passed the test. I had been allowed entry into the world of men.

## Oaks Sprung from Acorns

To speak of hunting and guns in this antiseptic age is to risk public approbation for political incorrectness. But for many young people who grew up in the country when I was a kid, hunting was both a pastime and an economic necessity—not to mention an excellent introduction to nature and the duties of adulthood. Hunting taught responsibility and self-reliance. We learned how to clean and care for our own guns. How to field dress game and prepare it for the table. How to read a compass and navigate the woods. We ate the game we shot and left behind no trash or trace of our presence in the woods except for our footsteps on the ground.

Hunting season began in September with migratory birds, moved to small game in October, and then to the big prize in November: white-tailed deer. Every weekend after Thanksgiving, my father would load up the car and take us four boys up north to the game lands of upstate Pennsylvania to sit in the frigid woods for hours at a time. We didn't see many deer, but we witnessed many a stunning sunrise, and the slow creep of dawn through the woods, and the drumming of the pileated woodpecker on a hollow trunk, and the gurgling of clear-flowing springs through fern-lined clefts.

My father had a stroke late in his life and didn't do much hunting for the last five or six years or so before he passed. But back in his day, he got out in the woods as much as his busy schedule allowed. To see him walking through the woods with a gun in his hands was to see the face of a man in love.

He is gone now, but more than forty years after he first put that gun in my arms, my father walks with me today as I stride through this stand of oak and hickory trees. I carry with me his legacy of resilience and self-determined individualism, just as I carry with me my mother's steadfast faith and optimism. Their blood courses through me, as does the blood of my namesake James Delano Kerr, and the blood of all of my ancestors.

We never walk alone, though it often feels that way. We are not one but many, a composite of all who have come before us, their collective will and intelligence, their struggles and victories in the face of adversities. We are oaks in a forest of oaks: tall, strong, deep-rooted, sprung from the acorns of a common past.

What do we have to fear?

# 15

# Rebellion of the Salt-Seeking Spirit

*A musician must make music, an artist must paint, a poet must write, if he is to be ultimately at peace with himself. What a man can be, he must be.*

—Abraham Maslow

I come out of the tunnel of the woods into the diminished light of a fast-dying day. I can feel the air growing colder. Sunset is coming on—I need to pick up my pace. I don't want to be walking these country roads in the dark.

Up ahead, I come to a dead end, where I turn left onto a road by the name of Callowhill. Up Callowhill half a mile, I turn right on Hilltown Pike. I am on the final stretch toward home. I have driven these roads so many times that I could plot out every twist and turn and pothole on Google Maps. But how much more I notice while walking them! What would sweep by my car window in a blur of shapes and colors now takes individual shape like a tapestry seen up close. I see a birdhouse in a side yard being visited by a couple of a cardinals. A "Kindness Lives Here" flag hangs beneath a mailbox. Goats graze in a pasture behind a barn. How many times have I driven this road and never noticed those goats!

Everything becomes clearer when you take it in slowly. If that's true for one person like me, how much truer must it be for an entire society? How much are we collectively missing in our hellbent race through our days? What nuances, what vital details? What mistakes are we making in the name of speed? What faulty assumptions do we make about people and situations that would vanish if we considered them in the slow, purposeful walk of awareness? Has our relentless push for greater efficiency led us to huge amounts of waste in the form of hurried assessments, rushed judgments, and inattention to detail?

## Breaking the Chains That Bind

One thing I know now for certain, even in the midst of all the uncertainty of my situation, is that I will no longer be owned by a job. I have learned that lesson from my father. I may end up working for another big company or I may not. If I do, I will work hard and do a good job, because that's important to me, but I will not allow myself to be a cog in a machine, a screw in a flywheel, a remora fish riding the back of a whale.

I want a different pace for my life. A more human pace.

I want something else, too.

I want salt.

I want more salt in my life. I want to shake it up. Shake up the routine. See new vistas beyond the limited view of a designated place on a leviathan's back. Pursue the dreams that have been clawing at me like neglected children: *Pay attention to us! We're your flesh and blood! Don't let us wither away in here!*

If I've learned anything from my close call with colon cancer and other near-death experiences in my past, it's that life is short and exceedingly fragile. We tend to think that our days will march on like faithful soldiers until we're old and on our deathbed, and only then will it all come to an end. But the truth is that everything we treasure and value about life can be taken away at any moment by an accident or unexpected diagnosis.

In the meantime, many of us are chained to routine jobs that put food on our tables but do not provide salt. We want something more than to be suckerfish on a whale or krill for an impersonal marketing campaign. We want to do what moves our spirits. There's a rebel within each of us that wants to toss away the routine and be free. As we dutifully go about our days doing what's expected of us, we inwardly rage against the chains that hold us back, even though we ourselves have put those chains on. We want to rip off those chains, and the masks, too: We want to rip them off and stand before the world and say, Look! This is me! Not that rules-following, policy-bound, check-the-box remora fish you know around the office, but me! Me!

I think about all the times in the past that I've sat at my office desk bored stiff by an hour-long conference call that was getting nothing done; or frustrated by being told, without being asked for my input, to do something that made absolutely no sense just because someone higher up says it must be done; or seething over a critical email lobbed in my direction by someone throwing me under the bus for their own mistakes—wanting at that moment to say the hell with it and get up from my desk and walk away, but not doing it, because, well, I had bills to pay, obligations to meet, responsibilities to fulfill.

I suspect that this, more than anything, is what Thoreau meant by saying that the mass of men lead lives of quiet desperation. The human spirit longs to be free. But the human spirit is lodged in a mortal body that needs and wants things. Every need and want is another link in the chains that bind us. The longer the list of needs and wants, the longer the chain.

It strikes me that my father probably would have liked Thoreau if they had lived at the same time. The two of them were alike in many ways. They were both rebels. They both railed against blind conformity to the ways of the herd. Thoreau vigorously opposed slavery and other social policies of his time that he saw as unjust. He even spent a night in jail for refusing to pay taxes that supported the war against Mexico that he opposed. Thoreau's essay on civil disobedience was hugely influential in the thinking of Gandhi; Martin Luther King, Jr.; and other proponents of nonviolent means of promoting social change. Even his decision to live in a simple cabin in the woods, at a time of rapid industrialization, was itself an act of rebellion.

My father never did anything quite like that, but he wasn't afraid of walking his own way and he never shied from challenging authority when needed. For years, even before he retired, he stayed close to local politics and would regularly attend township meetings to keep an eye on what the local authorities were up to. He did his research and would come to the meetings armed with a stack of paperwork to challenge the commissioners on their plans and thinking. No one was going to pull a fast one on him.

Of course, I remind myself, Thoreau was a bachelor. He never married, never had kids. It was easy enough for him to go and live in the woods by himself for two years. My father was in an entirely different situation. He had a family and all the responsibilities that come with one, and he was not going to walk away from those obligations.

Did my dad regret marrying and having a family? I wonder as I walk. Did he regret all the responsibilities, the ties, the financial obligations?

I don't think so. For all the hardships he faced while we were growing up, my father would not have traded the life he had for all the riches in the world. His family was his pride and joy, and the core of it was his marriage with my mother. The bond that the two of them forged during sixty-four years of marriage was the most precious gift they gave to their children. They showed us the power of love to endure the wind and rain and storms of adversity and continue standing.

*And you, too, Jim*, I think. As hard as it's been this past decade since the divorce, for all the struggles I've been through, for all the money I've paid out in alimony and child support and college payments, I would never trade my life with my children for all the riches in the world.

It's true. Of all the things I would do differently if I could live my life over again, I would never change my decision to have children. My three sons have added immense richness to my life, well beyond the things extra money might have bought me. Thoreau never experienced that side of life, and he was the poorer for it, in my opinion. While family adds financial chains to our lives, it also provides salt.

I enjoy that salt in my life. I just have to find a way to make the money I need to get my kids through college and into adulthood while finding a path toward my dreams.

## The Old Joy Rises

All of this brews in my head like a heady malt beer as I continue up the country road in the fading October daylight. I pass a farm on my left where a horse is out grazing. I give a little cluck out of the corner of my mouth and the horse turns to look and whinnies, just as our horse Lucky used to do on our farm when I was growing up. The memory warms me.

I walk up another half a mile, go around a curve, and step through a small tunnel of trees. On the other side, the land opens up into a broad vista of rolling pastures and soybean fields, rimmed in the distance by a dark ridgeline of hills.

I always look forward to this part of my drive home from the office. The majestic view never fails to lift my spirit, and that's especially so today when I'm seeing it on foot. The sun has dipped down below the rim of hills on the horizon, setting the sky ablaze in fiery streaks of pink and lavender.

I stop for a moment to soak it all in. I have witnessed many a gorgeous sunset on this road during my commutes home at this time of the evening, but this day I'm seeing it not from the seat-belted safety of a car, but as a walker on the road itself. I'm not just an observer of the landscape but a participant in it, and my changed vantage point is making all the difference in what I'm seeing and experiencing.

My eyes go to a large cumulus cloud floating through the middle of the fire like a ship. The underbelly of the cloud is lit bright white. I almost expect to see the figure of Jesus Christ riding at the helm of the cloud-ship. Closer in, I observe a herd of cattle grazing quietly in the dim-lit pasture. A swallow dips down low to the ground and then swoops upward again. A white church spire rises from an unseen hill in the distance. The evening stands suspended in a moment of beauty: the fiery sky, the grazing cattle, the swooping swallows, the golden soybeans awaiting harvesting. I feel like I've stepped into a painting.

What a gorgeous evening! How glorious to be alive on such a day!

And I am alive. I'm alive, and that's all that matters.

Something comes over me. It's the old joy I used to feel as a boy. It's been a while since I've felt it. Months. Maybe even years. But it hasn't left me. It was just covered up by the detritus of job stresses and financial worries and rush-hour commutes. The joy rises up my stomach, up my lungs, up my throat. Goosebumps break out across on my body, just like all those years ago when I was out picking raspberries and the wind swept through the trees overhead, lifting me up in a swell of elation.

## Voice of the Rebel Spirit

Along with the joy, I am aware of something else rising within me. It's the voice of my rebel spirit, seeking expression.

I know this voice. It's the same determined voice that carried me through hand surgery and eight months of physical therapy after my construction accident when I was nineteen—the voice that said: *I will not let this stop me.*

It's the same determined voice that carried me through the bewilderment and agony of my first bout of clinical depression when I was in my twenties, the voice that shouted back to the black beast when it told me I was hopeless: *No, it's not true! You will not have me!*

It's the same determined voice that carried me through those horrific years in my forties when my marriage was falling apart and the bottom fell out of the financial markets and the beast had me firmly again in its jaws and this time it seemed there truly wasn't any hope: *No, no, no! I won't give up. Never! Never! Never!*

It's the same determined voice that carried me through six grueling months of chemotherapy following my colon resection: sitting in that chair in the infusion room having those awful toxic chemicals pumped into my bloodstream, leaving me drained to the dregs with nothing else to go on except for that stubborn voice inside that said: *I will get through this! I have a lot more life to live.*

It's the same determined voice that always bids me to return to my writing when I've received yet another rejection from a faceless journal or publishing house that doesn't have time to read my submission but is happy to add me to the mailing list for its fall lineup of books—the voice that shouts back: *You're wrong! I do have talent! I will succeed!*

It sounds strange to think of myself as a rebel. Haven't I worked for the same company for twenty-eight years? Haven't I opted for the safety of attaching onto the back of a leviathan, rather than making my own way through the blue waters of the marketplace?

All of that is true. It was a choice I made because I loved my kids and wanted them to feel secure. But that doesn't change the longing in my heart to toss all of that safety aside and break free. That longing is real. I know so because I feel it, and feelings must be honored or else they get backed up, and I know all too well what happens when feelings get backed up. It's not pretty.

I need to listen more to that rebel voice inside me. Cultivate it. Follow it. See where it takes me.

I'm not young any longer, but I still have time. There's plenty of salt in the sea. I just need to go get it.

# 16

# The Quarry

*In the depth of winter, I finally learned that within me there lay an invincible summer.*

—Albert Camus

Moving on, I walk to the end of the cow pasture, where I turn left onto Blooming Glen Road, the road that will take me to the development where I live. The dark ridgeline of hills in the distance is drawing closer. My development is at the base of that ridge. I'm just a couple of miles from home now.

I need only stroll through the village of Blooming Glen and walk another mile up the road and I'll be there.

But before I do that, I have something to do. I want to pay a visit to a place right off the road here, a place by the name of Blooming Glen Quarry.

The quarry supplies crushed stone products for builders and landscapers in the area. I only ever visited it once many years ago when I stopped by to order a load of stone for a patio I was building. But an image of this place loomed large in my thoughts when I was at the deepest, darkest points of my despair. This quarry was the option my exhausted mind kept serving up to me back then as an escape from my unremitting pain.

I'm not exactly sure why my ego-mind saw a quarry as the solution, as opposed to, say, a gun, a rope, or a cocktail of sleeping pills. I'm a hunter, after all; I have plenty of guns and ammo handy. Perhaps my efficiency-seeking mind perceived the quarry as the easiest way to accomplish the task. Perhaps my father had so drilled safety into my head that I wouldn't consider a gun as an option. Or perhaps my mind was somehow entranced by the notion of taking that final self-determined act of sailing over the cliff in my car to my fate, à la Thelma and Louise.

All I know is that my ego-mind chose a quarry as the way out of my pain. And now, more than ten years on, I feel the need to take a look at the place and see if it looks anything like the image I have of it in my head.

# A View of Desolation

I advance stealthily through the twilight toward the entrance to the quarry. A chain-link fence runs around the perimeter of the quarry. The business is closed for the day, the front gate locked. Just inside the gate is a station for weighing the loads of trucks coming in and out of the quarry. I likely wouldn't have attempted to enter the quarry here at the main entrance. Too many obstructions. I would have chosen a more out-of-the-way spot.

I follow the chain-link fence line along the west rim of the quarry. The fence is about ten feet high and topped with a single curlicue of barbed wire. Strong enough to keep out a bunch of crazy kids out for an adventure, but not to stop a two-ton car going forty miles an hour.

A row of white pines follows the chain-link fence for a couple hundred yards. Where the pines end, I come to an old access road for construction vehicles. The stone road is choked with weeds and doesn't appear to be used much anymore. The access road is barred by a flimsy-looking gate. I walk up to the gate and check it out. The gate hangs crookedly on rusted hinges and is secured by a simple chain and padlock. On the other side of the gate, the road goes on for another fifteen feet or so before tumbling down to the quarry depths below.

This is it—this is the spot I would have chosen. There's enough runway for a car to build up a sufficient head of steam to bust right through this gate. I would have sailed to the bottom of that quarry carrying a load of twisted gate and barbed wire along with me.

I wrap my fingers through the cold chain-link fence and gaze out at the dark chasm like a prisoner contemplating freedom. The quarry isn't as wide and deep as I imagined it, and certainly not as pretty. In my mind I'd pictured a deep chasm cut through with layers of veined, multicolor stone. My image of a quarry must have gotten mixed up with all the pictures I've seen over the years of America's natural parks.

The fact is, a stone quarry is pretty ugly—at least a quarry like this one that mines for crushed stone. Thelma and Louise at least got a majestic final view of the red, gray, and mauve rock layers of the Grand Canyon before plunging to their end. All I would have gotten for my final view would have been gouged-out walls of bluish-gray shale and argillite.

This is where the ego-mind will take us if we leave it to its own device: a stark, ugly place. There's nothing romantic or redeeming about such an end, no matter how hard the ego tries to dress it up. The decision to end a life before its time for the sole purpose of ending pain is the most short-sighted decision the ego could ever make, and yet the ego-mind is so firmly attached to its fabricated identity and all the illusions that go with it that it's perfectly willing to destroy itself if those illusions prove unworkable. The ego-mind would rather give up on life itself than give up its identity.

It was spirit that saved me from that fate, just as it saved me during other tough passages in my life. But I could only be saved when my ego-mind was no longer in control, when I finally threw up my hands and surrendered to the spirit.

## Giving It over to God

As I look out at the dimly lit quarry, I recall a day when I was contemplating ending my life in this ugly pit.

It was a month or so after my skiing accident and I was sitting by myself out in my car in the parking lot of the corporate office. This was when things were at their worst in my divorce proceedings. I was out of the house, on crutches, living temporarily with my sister and brother-in-law. My wife and I were battling over custody arrangements for the children, and I was making regular trips to the family court offices for appearances.

Meanwhile, the financial markets were crashing in the Great Recession. Between my lawyer bills and the diving markets, I had lost most of my savings. To make matters worse, the company was restructuring again and laying off more workers. My world, inside and outside, felt bleak and hopeless.

Through sheer force of will, I had managed to keep my job through it all. Every morning I dragged myself out of bed to wade through another day of anguish. But I was at the end of my rope. I had been severely depressed for four years and felt I couldn't do it any longer. No one could say I hadn't tried to get better. I had worked so hard, but there was nothing else to try. I had exhausted all the possibilities. The beast had won.

And so, over lunch, I hobbled out on my crutches to my car and placed a call to my mother, who had been my constant companion through my many dark days. She was in her seventies now and I didn't want to burden her any longer with my troubles. But after all we'd been through together, I felt the need to get her permission to do what I was thinking about doing.

"I can't do this any longer, Mom," I said through tears. "I need you to let me go."

I felt the shock of my words go through her. She was quiet for a moment before replying in a shaken but firm voice. "Well, I can't let you go," she said.

"Please. Just tell me it's okay."

"I won't let you go, Jim," she repeated. "I don't know why God is putting you through this, but I believe there's a reason for it and I'm not going to give up on you. And neither is your father."

I hung up, without her blessing, and sat in the car. The demon voice spoke to me: *Do it, Jim.*

I looked down at the keys in the ignition.

*You're hopeless! Start the car. Get it over with!*

But I couldn't. I couldn't put those keys in the ignition. Through all the dark days and years I had spent in the teeth of the black beast, I had never heeded its call to hurt myself, and I couldn't do it now either. All the weights were tipped to the "Not to Be" side of my psychic scale, but the will to live within me was too strong.

And so, with that final option off the table, I threw up my hands. I reclined back on the car seat, looked up at the gray cloth roof, and said, "Lord, I give up. I don't know what kind of loving God would do this to one of his creatures, but I've tried everything, so whatever you plan to do with me, go ahead. I accept it. I have nothing else to give. I'm spent. I'm done."

I remember feeling at that moment an immense relief. It was as if a huge burden I'd been carrying my entire adult life was suddenly lifted from my shoulders. It was the burden of trying. I didn't have to try to fix myself anymore, because trying was clearly useless. And so I could put down my work gloves and tools and just . . . be. Faced with the stark choice between destroying myself or accepting myself, I chose to accept myself, just as I was, warts and all.

At that moment, my exhausted ego dropped its armor and left me defenseless as a shivering newborn mole. I lay there waiting to be gobbled up into oblivion. The beast that I had been trying to kill for twenty-five years came up to me, bared its teeth, gave a disinterested sniff, and then backed away. I watched it move off into the brush.

It wasn't going to kill me. I was not going to die.

I sat back up in the car seat and looked around. It was a warm spring day and through the open car windows, I heard birds chirping. A soft breeze blew through in the window, carrying smells of flowers and thawing earth.

For the first time in years, I felt at peace. I didn't know what was going to happen or how I was going to get out of this deep hole I was in, but I didn't have to worry about it anymore, because I wasn't in charge of figuring it out. God was in charge. I had given it over to Him, as my mother had been encouraging me to do.

I finally understood what she'd been saying all these months and years. I was on my way out of the tunnel, and God was carrying me.

## Rejecting the Lies of the Ego-Mind

A few weeks later, I moved out of my sister's house into the rental townhouse. Soon after, I had my magical cup of oatmeal and started the gratitude experiment. By the end of that summer, I was back in the land of the living.

As I look through the chain-link fence at the quarry, I'm filled with gratitude that I did not listen to my exhausted ego-mind that day when I sat out in the car contemplating suicide. How many of life's blessings would I have missed if I had listened to its mad talk and driven into the quarry of despair!

My recent brush with cancer aside, my life has been good over the past ten years. Very good, in fact. Sunday morning breakfasts and cookouts with my boys. Vacations and camping trips. College visits. Parties and get-togethers with my family. Wonderful times. I met my girlfriend and we have a wonderful relationship.

A decade ago, I didn't think any of this was possible. What a difference time can make if only we have faith, resilience, and a steely determination that we will not give up, however seemingly hopeless our present circumstances may be. I was in the darkest of places on that day sitting in my car in the parking lot at work. I was convinced there was no hope for me, that my circumstances were beyond repair, that I had exhausted all the options for ever getting to a place of peace and happiness.

But I was wrong. I wasn't hopeless at all. I had allowed myself to be misled by a puffed-up little ego that thought it was more powerful than life itself.

How many lives have been tragically cut short thanks to such misguided thinking? How many precious days have been lost, how many wonderful talents, how many hopes and dreams dashed to the rocks of despair by the workings of an ego-mind cut off from the voice of the spirit? There aren't enough quarries on this Earth to contain it all. I think of Anthony Bourdain, Kate Spade, Robin Williams, and other high-profile celebrities who have chosen the way of the quarry in recent years.

And it's not just the rich and famous. The despair is everywhere. Suicide rates are skyrocketing. We are in the midst of a raging opioid crisis. More people than ever before are suffering from depression, anxiety, and other emotional disorders. Mental-health facilities are filled to the brim. How could a country of such opportunities and material abundance be so miserably unhappy?

I am filled with an upwelling of empathy for everyone who is suffering the pain and darkness of detachment from spirit. I totally get why they would want to give up. It's because of the suffering. Unlike the illusions that produce it, suffering is very real. Pain is real. Depression is real. Anxiety is real. To reject any feeling, regardless of where it comes from, only makes the feeling more intense. Whatever you resist not only persists, but grows.

I get all that. But having been there myself, I can say with certainty that although the pain feels unbearable and permanent, it isn't. Despair, like all emotions, will pass if it is acknowledged, understood, and released. What makes despair stick is the way the ego-mind makes it part of a bigger story of misery and defeat, and all the defeating self-talk that goes with that story: *It's hopeless. There's something wrong with me. I'm broken, I'm defective, I'm not worthy.*

All of these things are lies—lies told by a controlling ego-mind caught up in its own delusions and frustrations that things aren't going its way. Don't believe them. Acknowledge them, smile at them the way you do with a pouting child, and then let them go. Why give credence to something that isn't true?

## The Quarry Is Not Our End

The quarry need not be our end. There is another way than the one offered up to us by the ego-mind. I think of the Longfellow poem that my father would go around the house quoting when we were growing up. He never read to us the full poem, only those memorable lines about "dumb, driven cattle" and "heroes in the strife." But shortly after my Dad passed away following a series of strokes, I tracked down the poem and read it in its entirety.

The poem is called "A Psalm of Life" and it begins this way:

> *Tell me not, in mournful numbers,*
>   *Life is but an empty dream!*
> *For the soul is dead that slumbers,*
>   *And things are not what they seem.*
> *Life is real! Life is earnest!*
>   *And the grave is not its goal;*

> *Dust thou art, to dust returnest,*
>
> *Was not spoken of the soul.*

Reading the lines in context, I realized that I misinterpreted what Longfellow was saying about heroes and cattle. I read the words as a call for achievement when I think they are saying something else altogether. They're saying life itself is real, not all the made-up stuff of the ego. Things are not as they appear to be in that empty fantasy world of the ego-mind. We are here for something much greater and more fulfilling than simply to achieve great things. We are here to enjoy the journey and help others along the way.

Perhaps that is what God has in mind for me now, in this new phase of my life: to use my gifts to help others who are suffering. Maybe I'll write a book about my life's journey, my frequent walks through the land of the black beast and how I finally found my way back to equanimity and peace.

Yes, I think I'll write about this day, too—this momentous day when I found out I'm going to be losing my job. I'll call the book *The Long Walk Home*.

That, too, is part of the story, after all.

My story.

Who better to tell it than me?

# 17

# Coming Home

*She was becoming herself and daily casting aside that fictitious self which we assume like a garment with which to appear before the world.*

—Kate Chopin

I stroll through the tiny village of Blooming Glen. Blink as you drive through Blooming Glen and you'll miss most of everything there is to see of this town. But walk through it as I'm doing now and you'll catch the quaintness of the place.

The post office looks like it's off a postcard from Smalltown, USA. The postmaster's name is Deb. She always has a smile for me when I walk through the doors with a package in my hand or when I'm in need of more Forever stamps. When the U.S. Postal Service—a leviathan in its own right—went through a cost-cutting consolidation a few years back, there was some concern around these parts that this little post office would close and Deb would lose her job. But the office made the cut and Deb continues to faithfully serve the people of this town, albeit with hours that seem to get more limited every year.

Beyond the post office, I walk past a line of pretty little Colonial houses decorated for Halloween. Jack-o-lanterns and skulls glow weakly through the dusk on the front porches among corn stalks and scarecrows. I remember how much I loved Halloween as a boy, digging through the basket of cast-off clothes for whatever outfit I could put together and setting out into the darkened streets to see how much of my bag I could fill with candy. When I had kids of my own, I loved taking them around on Halloween almost as much as when I trick-or-treated myself. There are treats in every season of our lives, if only we keep our eyes out for them.

## The Last Light of an October Day

I cross over Route 113—yet another three-number interstate road—and just like that, I'm out of Blooming Glen and on the final leg of my long journey home. I have walked more than twenty miles. That's a long way. I don't think I've walked twenty miles at one time since high school Senior Week in Ocean City, New Jersey, when my friends and I would walk the entire length of the beach while reciting lines from Teilhard de Chardin.

The sky above the ridgeline burns orange and pink with the last light of this beautiful fall day. What time is it? I don't wear a watch and haven't looked at my cell phone since I set out from the office. I slip my phone out of my pocket: 6:32 P.M.

I've been walking for six hours and twenty-six minutes. Four different people from the office have called me in that time, no doubt wondering where the heck I am. I wonder why I didn't hear their calls, then remember that I flicked off the phone ringer in a pique of disgust after getting the call from my boss.

I should really check my voice messages—my work emails, too—to see if there's anything urgent. But instead, I slip the phone back into my pocket and keep walking. Whatever issues I missed today will surely be there for me when I'm back in the office tomorrow. If people ask what happened to me, I'll tell them I had a family emergency. The company has gotten twenty-eight years of rock-solid reliable service from me. They can live with a disappearing act for one afternoon. I mean, what are they going to do—fire me?

Down a hill. Up a hill. Past the stately Mennonite church with the white steeple that I saw from a distance a mile or so back. Down another hill, along a field of recently harvested corn. I spot a handful of deer out in the gathering dusk, heads down, grazing on spent kernels.

Up ahead is the sign for my development. As I enter it, I feel like I've accomplished something, even though all I've really done is to take twenty times longer to get home than if I had driven my car. But I have cleared my head, and there's something to be said for that. I've cleared my head and I've cleared my soul and I'm feeling a lot better than I was when I walked out of the office at noon. My mind has quieted. The gnat cloud of worries has dissipated. I'm feeling more grounded, more centered. I am back in the spirit.

Isn't that the way it works with the spirit? We connect for a while, feel good and happy, and then the ego-mind takes us away into its make-believe world of straining and striving and wanting to be anywhere but where we are. It's a constant process of arriving and getting lost again, reconnecting and disconnecting.

But the more mindful we become, the more of our precious days we get to spend in the peaceful realm of the spirit and the less we waste in the messy, frantic, chaotic land of the mind. It's about conscious awareness. We catch ourselves beginning to worry and say, "Wait, I don't want to go there because I know it feels bad, because life is short and time is precious and I don't want to waste it wallowing in the muck."

That is the ultimate journey, isn't it—the journey to ourselves? The journey of coming to know our innermost desires and drives, our impulses and fears, the dreams that keep us going and the beliefs that keep us from going after those dreams. That's where home lies. Home is more than the physical place where we live. It's that inner place where we are free to be our true selves, where we don't have to pretend any longer, where we are doing what we love and being who we are intended to be.

Around the cul-de-sac and there it is, my lovely Cape Cod house. Yeah, I overpaid for it, but it's a really great house.

I'm fortunate to have such a nice place to raise my kids. I'm going to enjoy it while I have it, and then, when the kids are out of college . . . well, we'll see.

What a long, strange journey it's been! Fifty-five years of walking. It feels good to be home.

I'll need to call an Uber to get a lift back to the office so I can pick up my car. But first I'm going to sit for a while on my front-porch rocker. To tell the truth, I'm kind of tired.

# Postscript: New Beginnings

*Every wall is a door.*

—Ralph Waldo Emerson

Soon after informing me of my pending layoff, my manager himself left the company for greener pastures. Apparently, he'd had enough of the place, too.

His exit complicated the search for my successor, and I ended up staying for another two and a half months. My last day was a Friday in early January. I had already emptied my office and it was just a matter of pulling up my car to the side entrance, loading up a few boxes of personal items, and saying good-bye to my colleagues and friends.

It's an odd feeling, leaving an organization where you've worked for twenty-eight years and knowing you will never be back. It's like walking away from a long marriage that's gone sour and yet, even amid the bitterness of the divorce, you remember the good times, the experiences, all the things you've learned. You realize that some of your best years were spent in that marriage and you'll never get them back. You mourn the loss. You feel nostalgia.

And then there's the uncertainty. You have been tethered to this relationship for so long and now the cord has been cut and you're not sure what you're supposed to do. You feel both afraid and excited at the same time.

For years of my life, I was uncomfortable with fear and the feelings it engendered within me, until I came to understand that fear and excitement are the same energy, only they move in opposite directions. Fear comes from the archaic lizard part of our brain and flows inward, seeking to protect the self from perceived harm. Excitement comes from the spirit and flows outward, seeking to propel the self into brave new worlds of adventure and opportunity. Excitement is fear turned inside out. Feel fear and you know you are rich in energy. You just need to turn it outward to make it productive.

That's what I was thinking that morning as I drove away from the leviathan for the last time. I had gone through the seven stages of grief and had reached a place of peace with what was happening to me. I was now fifty-six years old and had no job lined up yet, but the truth was, I really didn't want one yet. I needed time to clear out the toxins in my head before jumping into something else. I had been given an exit package—nothing exorbitant, but enough to last me a few months until I figured out what I wanted to do.

I had time. I had faith.

It felt strange being at home in those days and weeks. When you've been leaving the house for work at the same time every morning for nearly thirty years, it's jarring to wake up on a workday morning and realize you have no particular obligation to be anywhere that day. Where's the email box that tells me what I need to be doing? Where's the calendar of calls I need to be on?

I was determined, however, to keep up my routine. Routines are vitally important for our health and happiness. They keep the mind focused and the spirit energized. I continued to get up at the same early hour to go to the gym for my morning workouts. I set a schedule for myself every day as to what I wanted to get done. I fixed up my home office. I did projects around the house that I'd not had time for while working.

And I wrote—a lot. I resurrected a long-dormant novel and started working on it again. I launched a blog called *Peaceable Man*, to tell of my journey through depression and adversity, in the hopes that it would help inspire other men struggling with similar issues. I wrote poems. I started outlining the idea for this book, which I didn't know much about other than that it would be about my long walk home that October day when I got the news of my great letting-go.

I knew I couldn't continue with this routine forever. I had a mortgage to pay. I had two sons in college and another about to start. Under the divorce settlement, I was responsible for my kids' medical insurance. I would need to get another job.

But I really didn't want to jump into the wrong thing. For a couple of months, I did some marketing consulting work for a good friend to help her promote her specialty medical practice. I enjoyed the work, enjoyed seeing the immediate results of my labor, and I toyed for a while with the idea of starting my own marketing consulting business to help small businesses grow. But I knew it would take me a few years to get that sort of thing off the ground and I had immediate financial needs—particularly those big college bills.

My exit package included the services of a job outplacement firm, which I took full advantage of. I went to job search classes and networking events. I scoured LinkedIn and job boards and began applying for jobs, but selectively. One thing I knew: Wherever I worked next, whatever I ended up doing, I was determined to avoid having to make a long commute every day. I would sacrifice my income before I did that again. The added stress wasn't worth it.

I knew, too, that whatever job I chose next would be temporary. I was loving the feeling of writing again, of having dedicated morning time to focus on writing creatively. The novel was going well. The blog posts were flowing out of me. It didn't even feel like work—I just put my fingers on the keyboard and let the words flow. I had all these book and story and poem ideas that I wanted to get down. I had an image of the life I wanted as an independent author and a marketing consultant.

It would take some time to get there, but I was determined to do it. I would fulfill my obligations to my boys until they were done college, and then I was going to make the jump. I would heed Thoreau's call to simplify, simplify! Downsize, sell the house, dump the mortgage, get rid of all debt, and save enough money so I could be free to pursue my dreams.

I saw that path ahead of me. I had a plan. I just needed to find the job that would carry me through these next few transitional years.

***

Within three months of leaving the company, I found that job.

Through a friend, I found out about an opening at a financial technology company based in Florida. Several of my former colleagues, including a former boss, now worked there and they raved about the company. The firm was growing like a weed, profitable, and had an employee-friendly culture.

I put in my resumé, had a couple of interviews, and was offered the position. The pay was nearly the same as what I was making before, and the benefits were better. Best of all, I could work from home. After getting the news of the offer, I went out into the living room and did a little dance.

I worked for this new company for a few years, during which time the firm made a couple of huge acquisitions, tripled in revenue, and jumped into the rarified air of the Fortune 300. It was now a super-leviathan with more than fifty thousand employees and twelve billion dollars in revenue. It was gratifying to be working for a winner, and to see my work make a difference in the company's reputation and growth.

But I had dreams to go after. When my boys were out of college and on their own, I sold my beautiful Cape Cod house and used the equity to finally build that mountain cabin I'd long dreamed about. With no mortgage and no debt, I was able to slash my expenses and radically save until I had enough to cut the cord with the new company and go off on my own.

I could have worked there for another four or five years until I retired, and made a lot of money doing so. But these were critical years ahead. I had books to write—at least three or four of them that have been gestating in my head for a long time. It was now or never. I wasn't young anymore, and though I was thankfully still cancer-free and in good health, there were no guarantees. I had seen too many people wait until they turned sixty-five to go do things they wanted to do, only to have their golden years cut short by illness or disability. I had fulfilled my obligations and I didn't want to wait any longer to take a shot at my dreams.

Time, not money, is our most precious resource, and I wanted to spend what healthy years I had left to write, to see the world, to spend time with the people I loved. And as for money—I wasn't too worried. I had lowered my monthly expenses to a point where I could cover them between my savings and investments. If need be, I would do consulting on the side to help cover the cost of my medical insurance.

And hey, maybe one of my books would be a bestseller. The important thing is to give it a shot. The important thing—in the words of Henry David Thoreau—is not to get to the end of my life and realize I didn't live at all.

It's never too late to take a shot at your dreams.

Age is but a number.

The sun is but a morning star.

Go for it. Go for it all. Just make sure you enjoy the walk along the way.

*Praise you, Lord. Praise you.*

# References

1. The world's broken workplace. (2017, June 13). *The Chairman's Blog, Gallup.* Retrieved from https://news.gallup.com/opinion/chairman/212045/world-broken-workplace.aspx?g_source=position1&g_medium=related&g_campaign=tiles

2. Why Americans are more likely to work for a large employer, in 20 charts. (2017, April 6). *The Wall Street Journal.* Retrieved from https://www.wsj.com/graphics/big-companies-get-bigger/; U.S. Census Bureau. (2012). Statistics of U.S. Businesses. Retrieved from https://www.shrm.org/hr-today/news/hr-magazine/Documents/g12-susb.pdf

3. The astonishing human potential wasted on commutes. (2016, February 25). *The Washington Post.* Retrieved from https://www.washingtonpost.com/news/wonk/wp/2016/02/25/how-much-of-your-life-youre-wasting-on-your-commute/?%20noredirect=on

# Appendix: The Marketing Funnel

Different marketers use different terms to describe the buyer's journey from awareness to purchase, but the fundamental steps of the sales funnel haven't changed much since the concept was first introduced by advertising pioneer Elias St. Elmo Lewis at the turn of the twentieth century. What has changed is the sophistication of the marketing technology used to automate every stage of the funnel. The funnel looks something like this:

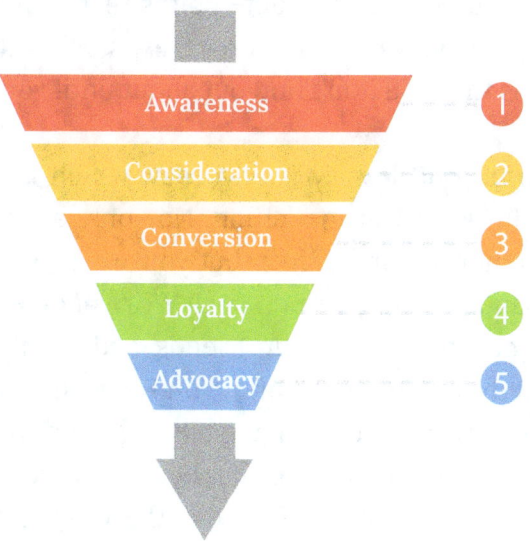

The first step is awareness: Grab our attention by whatever means possible to make us aware of the brand and lure us into the selling funnel.

The second step is consideration: Get us to consider the brand when we're in the market for something in a particular product category.

Third step is conversion: Convince us to take the next step of pulling out our credit card and buy the product. This is generally done by making us think we will not be hip, complete, or safe if we don't have this product in our lives, and then closing the sale by offering up an incredible deal that no reasonable person could ever refuse.

The fourth step is about cementing the deal by making us loyal, long-term customers. Now we've sold you, but we want you to keep coming back for more. So, we entice you to offer up your email address and sign up for our loyalty programs for the purpose of showering you with reward points whenever you buy our product—points that you can use for future trips or stays or gas purchases, albeit with a lot of restrictions that you don't find out about until you try to use them.

A step beyond loyalty is advocacy, which is nirvana to anyone who works in marketing. Not only are you now a loyal customer of our product, but you are also an advocate for the brand. It's become personal. We're buddies. You recommend our brand to your friends and family. You say wonderful things about our brand on Facebook and Twitter. You share pictures of us hanging out together on Instagram and tell stories of how your life has been made so much more convenient and complete because of this brand's product or service that you have come to love as much as your dog.

There are countless books on the marketing sales funnel if you'd like to learn more. One that I would recommend is *Invisible Selling Machine* by Ryan Deiss.

# Further Reading

The journey to inner peace begins with knowledge. By coming to understand the complex ways that our thoughts, perceptions, core beliefs, and past experiences and traumas work together to affect how we feel on a day-to-day basis, we move from being victims of our moods to manifesters of our own reality.

The good news is that there are plenty of great books out there to help guide us in this journey to self-understanding. Here are a few that have helped me immensely in my own journey to inner peace.

***The Power of Now: A Guide to Spiritual Enlightenment***, by Eckhart Tolle (New World Library, 2004). A must-read. Written in a simple question-and-answer format, this modern-day classic takes us by the hand and leads us step by step down the path to living a life of inner peace and tranquility.

***Full Catastrophe Living (Revised Edition): Using the Wisdom of Your Body and Mind to Face Stress, Pain and Illness***, by Jon Kabat-Zinn (Bantam, 2013). Originally published in 1990, this seminal book from Kabat-Zinn, founder of the Stress Reduction Clinic at the University of Massachusetts, is packed with wisdom on how to identify the sources of stress in our lives and better navigate them through meditation and daily "mindfulness" training.

***Wherever You Go, There You Are: Mindfulness Meditation in Everyday Life***, by Jon Kabat-Zinn (Hachette Books, 2005). First published in 1994, this hugely influential and popular book from Kabat-Zinn, which followed *Full Catastrophe Living*, has introduced millions of people to the healing power of mindfulness.

***The Four Agreements: A Practical Guide to Personal Freedom***, by Don Miguel Ruiz (Amber-Allen Publishing, 2018). Originally published in 1997, this book has sold more than 10 million copies and changed many people's lives by laying out "four agreements" to leading a more peaceful life.

***Feeling Good: The New Mood Therapy***, by David D. Burns (William Morrow, 1999). Published in 1980 and reprinted a number of times since, this book has been instrumental in popularizing cognitive-based approaches for the treatment of depression, anxiety, and other mood conditions.

***Flourish, Authentic Happiness, & Learned Optimism*** (3-Book Collection) by Martin Seligman (Nicholas Brealey Publishing, 2019). In this three-book collection, the father of the modern school of positive psychology walks through his theories on learned optimism, happiness, and well-being—and how we can actively create them in our lives.

***The Untethered Soul: The Journey Beyond Yourself***, by Michael A. Singer (New Harbinger Publications, 2007). The spiritual teacher and founder of the nondenominational meditation center Temple of the Universe takes us on a tour of inner consciousness that reframes the way we think about the problems in our lives.

***The Highly Sensitive Person: How to Thrive When the World Overwhelms You***, by Elaine Aron (Broadway Books, 1997). If you are easily overstimulated and struggle with emotions that sometimes feel too big for you, this book could change your life and your way of viewing yourself.

***If You Feel Too Much, Expanded Edition: Thoughts on Things Found and Lost and Hoped For***, by Jamie Tworkowski (TarcherPerigee, 2016). This poetic, beautifully written collection of personal vignettes will move and inspire anyone who is walking through the lonely darkness of depression.

***A Course in Miracles: Combined Volume***, by Helen Schucman (Foundation for Inner Peace, 1976). This cult classic provides a self-study course in how we manifest our own realities in life.

***The Ten Best-Ever Anxiety Management Techniques: Understanding How Your Brain Makes You Anxious and What You Can Do to Change It***, by Margaret Wehrenberg (W. W. Norton & Co., 2018). This book, written by the author of *The Anxious Brain*, provides a comprehensive, easy-to-read guide to understanding what is going on in your body when you're anxious, and the best techniques for getting out of the maze.

***Meditation for Life***, by Martine Batchelor (Wisdom Publications, 2001). Written by a former Buddhist nun, this book is an accessible, easy-to-read, and often funny guide to the practice of meditation for the beginner.

**The Miracle of Mindfulness: An Introduction to the Practice of Meditation**, by Thich Nhat Hanh (Beacon Press, 1999). An excellent introduction into meditation and mindfulness by the Vietnamese-born monk and Zen master.

Also highly recommended from the amazingly prolific Thich Nhat Hanh: **The Heart of the Buddha's Teaching: Transforming Suffering into Peace, Joy, and Liberation** (Harmony, 1999). Another excellent primer into Buddhism and Eastern enlightenment practices.

**The Myth of Freedom and the Way of Meditation**, by Chogyam Trungpa (Shambhala, 2002). The late meditation master distills Buddhist teachings in accessible language that is easy to follow and apply in our daily lives.

**When Things Fall Apart: Heart Advice for Difficult Times**, by Pema Chodron (Shambhala, 2016). This beautiful book brings together wisdom from some of Chodron's most powerful and instructive talks.

## Oldies but Goodies

**Hope and Help for Your Nerves**, by Claire Weekes (Berkley, 1990). Despite somewhat dated language (it was written in the 1960s), this book is gold for anyone suffering from severe anxiety, panic attacks, or is agoraphobic and housebound.

***As a Man Thinketh***, by James Allen (public domain). This little masterpiece, published by Englishman James Allen in 1902, hammers home the message that our thoughts, and nothing else, determine our success and happiness in life.

***Byways of Blessedness***, by James Allen (public domain). Written in 1904, this is a classic guide to cultivating right states of mind and wise modes of action that yield peace and joy.

***Psycho-Cybernetics: Updated and Expanded***, Dr. Maxwell Maltz (TarcherPerigee, 2015). Considered one of the greatest self-help books of all time, this book (first published in 1960) contains sage advice and practical techniques for mastering the mind and replacing destructive old mental scripts with more helpful stuff.

***The Miracle of Right Thought***, by Dr. Orison Swett Marden (public domain). Originally published in 1910, this little book has been greatly influential on many twentieth-century businesspeople and writers, from Dale Carnegie to Anthony Robbins.

# About the Author

James Kerr led award-winning global communications and PR programs at a number of Fortune 500 technology companies before leaving the corporate world to pursue his passion for writing. His fiction and poetry have appeared in the *Sewanee Review*, *Red River Review*, *The Poet*, *Short Story Town*, and other journals. He writes on fatherhood, men's health, and the path of the inner warrior in his blog *Peaceable Man*.

*The Long Walk Home* is his first published book. When not writing, you'll find him fishing, hiking, or out exploring with his German Shorthaired Pointer Cassie near his home in the Endless Mountains of Pennsylvania.

# About the Illustrator

Alyssa Beard is an architecture student at Rensselaer Polytechnic Institute. She lives in Doylestown, Pennsylvania.

www.ingramcontent.com/pod-product-compliance
Lightning Source LLC
Chambersburg PA
CBHW052135070526
44585CB00017B/1840